ERASMUS OF ROTTERDAM

Erasmus of Rotterdam

A Quincentennial Symposium

Edited by
Richard L. DeMolen

TWAYNE PUBLISHERS, INC.: NEW YORK

Foreword

WELCOME ADDRESS:

THE ERASMUS SYMPOSIUM
October 27 and 28, 1969

By ROBERT M. DAVIES

Ladies and gentlemen, as Provost of Ithaca College, I am delighted to welcome each of you, most cordially indeed, to the 500th anniversary of the birth of Desiderius Erasmus (1469–1536).

At the outset, it seems appropriate to note that in doing so, we join eleven other institutions in Europe and America which are celebrating in various ways the birth of the great humanist scholar whom we seek to help revitalize our lives. Of these celebrations, one is in France, six in Belgium, one in the Netherlands, two others here in the United States, at the Folger Shakespeare Library, and the University of Notre Dame, and, quite interestingly, one in the Soviet Union to be celebrated in September, 1970. It should also be mentioned here that in the true spirit of humanistic scholarship, Cornell University has most graciously loaned to Ithaca College some of the most prized items in its notable Erasmus collection. We are, of course, most grateful for this generous cooperation from Cornell University and I should like to encourage each of you to inspect these items on display in the Ithaca College library.

As you have noticed from the program schedule, it is my pleasant responsibility to extend this welcome to you and to introduce the participants in the symposium. In extending my welcome, I should like, first of all, to make a personal comment and then a more general comment on behalf of the College. On the purely personal level, I do not believe that any public function I have performed here at Ithaca College has given me a more genuine sense of gratification than being able to welcome you to this symposium. While my own graduate work in English at the University of Pennsylvania was in large measure done in the field of British literature, when it came time to address myself to a topic of research for my dissertation, I finally selected an American literary critic—Paul Elmer More—who was one of the two leaders of that movement in the 1920s which came to be called the New Humanist Movement. In consequence, for nearly a decade of my life, I was deeply involved in the study of humanism and will say simply that I believe the results of that work have entered into my life in ways that may not always be true of one's dissertation. During those days, I came to realize how very rich is that stream of scholarship which in one form or another is related to what we call humanism. It would certainly not be appropriate for me to elaborate on what I learned in that study, but those of you who have spent so many hours in the company of other humanists, both in speech and in written word, will understand, I am sure, how sincere is the word of welcome from one humanist to another.

On a somewhat broader note, I am particularly happy as well to welcome you to Ithaca College, because of the unique nature of one of our notable curricular components. Here at Ithaca College, we are very proud of a program which we call the Triplum. Essentially, the Triplum represents a major commitment on the part of our faculty and students to the values and traditions of the world of humanism, for the Triplum includes three years of work in philosophy, literature, and history, representing in all 54 hours of semester credits for those who enroll in this program. As far as I can tell, this is about double or even triple the kind of curricular commitment that is generally included in humanistic studies in most institutions, and we make this commitment at Ithaca College in the belief that such learning from the past has much significant meaning for the world today.

One additional note seems to be appropriate. Clearly, what we are engaged in here today is an act of folly. A fugitive quotation by some learned historian recently asserted that quite likely nothing that happened to humanity prior to World War I has relevance for the modern world. If it be true that those of us over thirty are not to be trusted and have little to say to those under thirty, how foolish it must seem to refer to the words of a man who amplifies the generation gap at least fifteen-fold. Perhaps, what we are doing here is totally irrelevant. If so, it may be an act of folly, and we are joined here today in praising folly.

In thinking of the education of young people who will live thirty years from now, I have sometimes mused on the question, Will the changing world change humanity? It is an intriguing possibility as we consider the impact of television, the possibility of genetic control, the enormously intensified possibilities of human mobility, human learning, and the like. But there is another question akin to this. Has the changing world changed humanity in the past?

And it is in answering this question that we look with most assurance to the future. For surely, the changing world of the past has not markedly changed humanity; and it may be questioned whether the changing world of the future will change humanity then. Does anyone here feel, for example, that Desiderius Erasmus would not find scintillating things to say about the kaleidoscopic world of television; wise and witty reflections on many sophomoric educational efforts; pungent comments on our aimless society with its shallow heart and meretricious glitter!

Most cordially, therefore, may I both welcome and present to you the four Erasmian scholars who will be speaking to us over the next two days: Dr. Albert Hyma, Professor Emeritus of History, from the University of Michigan; Dr. James D. Tracy, Assistant Professor of History, from the University of Minnesota; Dr. Lewis W. Spitz, Professor of History, Stanford University, and Dr. John C. Olin, Professor of History, Fordham University.

Finally, with some satisfaction, with much sadness, and with great respect, I should report that the papers given at this symposium are to be published in collected form and that the resulting volume will be dedicated to the memory of the late Dr. John B. MacInnes, Professor of History at Ithaca College and Chairman of the History Department for half a dozen years. Like Erasmus, Professor MacInnes was a Christian scholar and humanist. We are impoverished by his death, but enriched by his memory, and to that memory we dedicate this symposium.

Preface

The idea of holding an Erasmus Symposium at Ithaca College to commemorate the quincentennial of the birth of the Prince of Humanists was first suggested by Professor Albert Hyma of the University of Michigan during a visit to Ithaca, New York, in the fall of 1968. On that occasion, he fondly recalled the varied events of the 1936 Rotterdam Congress, marking the four-hundredth anniversary of the Dutch savant's death, which captured his imagination and stimulated his later scholarship. With the enthusiastic support of Professor Robert A. Ryan, chairman of the department of history, and Dr. Robert M. Davies, provost, the concept of an Ithaca College symposium took shape. October 27 and 28 were designated as the most appropriate time for the celebration because Professor Hyma had argued convincingly in his book *The Youth of Erasmus* that Erasmus was born in Rotterdam on the eve of October 28, 1469.

The selection of the lecture topics for the Erasmus Symposium was the responsibility of the director, but he was assisted in his choice of participants by Professor Craig R. Thompson of the University of Pennsylvania. In this connection, the director suspects that the spontaneity of the principal speakers in accepting his original invitation rests with Professor Thompson's silent endorsement, and he gratefully acknowledges his indebtedness. The success of the Ithaca College Symposium, however, was due to the speakers themselves: Professors Albert Hyma, James D. Tracy, Lewis W. Spitz and John C. Olin shared their erudition and wit with cordial generosity.

With one exception, all of the papers which were presented at Ithaca College are published here. We have decided to omit Professor Hyma's lecture from this volume because it has recently been published elsewhere.* In its place, we are pleased to offer

---

*Albert Hyma, "The Contributions by Erasmus to Dynamic Christianity" in *Scrinium Erasmianum.* . . . ed. by Joseph Coppens (Leiden: E. J. Brill, 1969), Vol. 2, pp. 106–131.

a paper given by Professor Richard J. Schoeck of the University of Toronto at the University of Notre Dame on December 13, 1969. Like the other lectures it carries forward, quite admirably, the theme of Ithaca College's symposium.

In the pages which follow, the authors attempt, each in his own way, to present an image of Erasmus which combines elements of the *Devotio Moderna* and Italian humanism. They try to clarify his significant role in the Renaissance of the North; and, above all, they seek to focus attention on the uniqueness of his contribution. Erasmus was not merely a precursor of religious revolutionaries like Luther and Calvin, nor an early devotee of seventeenth century rationalism, nor even a man on horseback, caught between two opposing camps. Instead, he was a reformer in his own right. As the proponent and originator of a philosophy of reform, he sought to bridge two worlds, those of patristic Christianity and sixteenth-century society, in order to effect a new and more humane world order.

In the preparation of the symposium lecturers for publication, the editor relied upon the advice of three members of his department: Professors Richard J. Daly, Patricia P. Hickin, and Donald L. Niewyk gave unstintingly of their time and counsel. To these scholars and to the countless, thoughtful expressions of encouragement from the participants themselves, the editor expresses his appreciation.

RICHARD L. DEMOLEN

The Folger Shakespeare Library
March 2, 1970

Table of Contents

Chronology

October 27, 1469: Erasmus was born at Rotterdam, the second son of Gerard, a priest, and Margaret, a domestic servant.

1473 to 1484: At the age of four, Erasmus, along with his older brother, Peter, was sent to school at Gouda. Later on he spent a year in Utrecht as a chorister and studied at Deventer, where he came under the influence of the Brethren of the Common Life from 1475 to 1484.

1484 to 1493: Following the death of his parents in 1484, Erasmus was sent by guardians to the Brethren School at s'Hertogenbosch. After three years in residence, he joined the Order of Canons Regular of St. Augustine and entered their monastery at Steyn in 1487. He was ordained to the priesthood on April 25, 1492, and remained at Steyn until 1493.

1493 to 1500: A year after his ordination, Erasmus was appointed Latin secretary to Henry of Bergen, the Bishop of Cambrai, and when the bishop's proposed trip to Italy failed to materialize, Erasmus was sent to Montaigu College within the University of Paris in 1495 to study theology. Short of funds, Erasmus found it necessary to tutor young men in Latin and in this way formed a friendship with the English nobleman William Blount. He also accepted the latter's invitation to visit England in 1499 and settled at Oxford where he met John Colet, Thomas Linacre, William Grocyn, and Thomas More.

1500 to 1505: Erasmus traveled in France and the Low Countries, preparing his first edition of the *Adages* (1500) and publishing the *Enchiridion Militis Christiani* (1503) and Lorenzo Valla's *Annotations on the New Testament* (1505).

1505 to 1509: Erasmus made his second visit to England in 1505 and spent five months at Oxford, London and, perhaps, Cambridge. Traveling to Italy, he accepted a doctor of divinity degree from the University of Turin in September of 1506.

From 1506 to 1509, Erasmus remained in Italy: first at Bologna and later at Venice, where he met Aldus Manutius, the scholar-printer.

1509 to 1514: Erasmus returned to England during this period. Through the influence of More, Archbishop William Warham and Bishop John Fisher, he was appointed Lady Margaret Professor of Divinity at Cambridge and a lecturer in Greek in 1511.

1514 to 1521: Erasmus was coaxed from Cambridge by Johann Froben, the prince of printers. Living for a few months at Basel in 1514, he served as editor of the works of St. Jerome and the New Testament. During the seven years which followed, he traveled widely in Holland and Germany, and even managed trips to England in 1515 and 1517. From 1517 to 1521 he resided in Louvain, helping to establish the Collegium Trilingue.

1521 to 1536: Erasmus returned to his retreat at Basel in 1521 and for eight years he acted as the general editor of Froben's press; but the acceptance of the reformation by that city in 1529 forced him to settle in Freiburg, where he lived for six years. In August of 1535, he traveled to Basel to edit the works of Origen.

July 12, 1536: Erasmus died at Basel, Switzerland, in the home of Jerome Froben, the son of his old friend.

Erasmus of Rotterdam in Profile

By RICHARD L. DeMOLEN

Richard L. DeMolen, the director of the Erasmus Symposium, graduated from the University of Michigan where he was a Horace H. Rackham Fellow and a member of Phi Beta Kappa and Phi Kappa Phi. Prior to his appointment to Ithaca College in 1967, Dr. DeMolen taught at Crowder College and Drury College. Among other publications, he is the editor of two forthcoming Renaissance studies: Houghton Mifflin has commissioned a collection of essays, which will be prepared by specialists in early modern Europe; and Teachers College Press will issue an abridged edition of Richard Mulcaster's *Positions* (1581) as part of its classics in education series.

Desiderius Erasmus is without question one of the most eminent figures of the sixteenth century. His life was one of periodic movement and controversy, and his fame, which was established in his own lifetime, has never suffered from critical appraisal. The reasons for Erasmus's popularity are not far to seek. In the words of Peter Gay, "Erasmus was a true classical spirit in his search for clarity and simplicity, a modern in his complexity, an ancestor of the Enlightenment in his critical temper and pacific cosmopolitanism. But, above all, he was a Christian intellectual, striving, as he himself said, to establish a *philosophia Christi.*" [1] Erasmus was in search of a new way of life, a code of behavior which would combine the best of Christianity and Renaissance humanism. And in this quest for truth and human understanding, he produced a copious array of practical and scholarly works. Together, they offered the Renaissance reader both a critical standard of composition and comparison and brilliant insights into intellectual and social progress. Great, indeed, were his services to posterity; but his origins, by contrast were most inauspicious.

Exactly five hundred years ago, on October 27, 1469, Desiderius Erasmus was born in Rotterdam, the second son of a cleric,

Gerard, and a serving maid named Margaret.[2] Because of the scandal attached to his parents' illicit relationship, Erasmus bore the scars of illegitimacy throughout life. Sensitive and introspective by nature, he must have been sorely humiliated when he accidentally witnessed the retelling of those unpleasant circumstances which surrounded his birth. Is it any wonder, then, that Erasmus sought comfort in lies and tried to disguise his origins by altering dates and exaggerating circumstances?[3]

At the age of four, Erasmus, along with his brother Peter, was sent to a privately conducted elementary school in Gouda. Later on he spent a year in Utrecht as a chorister in the cathedral. When he was about six, Erasmus began his studies at Deventer where he came under the influence of the Brethren of the Common Life and where he learned to master the elementary rules of Latin grammar. Following the untimely death of his parents in 1484, Erasmus was left in the care of indifferent guardians who, in an effort to rid themselves of their charge and, at the same time, to benefit from the meager trust fund which his father had established, sent him to the Brethren school at s'Hertogenbosch. After three years in residence, Erasmus joined the Order of Canons Regular of St. Augustine and entered their monastery at Steyn in 1487. He seems to have entered the religious life without really having considered the consequences. He himself suggested later on that his vocation had been promoted under pious pretenses by greedy guardians, and, therefore, doubted that he had a true calling.[4] But even in the face of these doubts, Erasmus professed solemn vows and was ordained to the priesthood. Following his ordination on April 25, 1492, the young priest remained at Steyn, leading the life of a choir monk and digesting selected morsels from the monastery's library. For at least one more year, he seemed satisfied with the Augustinians. He read widely in the classic and the patristic literature and developed a special appreciation of St. Jerome, the compiler of the Latin Vulgate edition of the Bible, and Lorenzo Valla, that erudite exposer of forged documents. Inspired by his confreres, he even wrote a treatise in defense of monasticism, which he called *On the Contempt of the World*. As an Augustinian Canon, Erasmus reflected the piety of his former teachers in Deventer and s'Hertogenbosch. These members of the Brethren of the Common Life were disciples of Christ who sought to imitate the Prince of Peace and to cultivate a spirit which we have learned to

call the *Devotio Moderna*.[5] Yet, at the same time, Erasmus also
came under the spell of Renaissance humanism. At Steyn, especially, he read voraciously in the classics and perfected a fluid and
lucid style of writing. Torn between the piety of the *Devotio
Moderna* and the humanism of Italy, he set his confused mind to
work on the *Book Against the Barbarians*. Written in the form
of dialogues, the tract expresses Erasmus's continuing respect for
monasticism but reveals a much stronger attraction to humanism.
Later on, he was to rewrite certain sections of the treatise in an
effort to expose the evils of the church and of the monastic life in
particular.[6] But in 1492, Erasmus was very much under the influence of the religious discipline of an Augustinian order and the
Brethren of the Common Life. Even so, he soon found the holy
rule and the confinement of the monastery to be exceedingly oner-
ous and longed for a glimpse of the Italian setting of which he had
only a reader's imperfect knowledge.

A year after his ordination, Erasmus discovered an episcopal
patron who was willing to free him from the monastic cell and
from the responsibilities of community life. Moreover, since this
princely bishop promised him a year's residence in Rome and
future opportunities for study, how could he resist? In the face of
such tempting prospects, Erasmus accepted an appointment in
1493 as Latin secretary to Henry of Bergen, the bishop of Cambrai. But only disappointment followed his decision. Within a
month, the bishop's proposed trip to Italy, where he had hoped
to be invested as a cardinal, failed to materialize and Erasmus
feared that he would be required to return to Steyn and there
resume the monastic life for which he had developed contempt.
But his fears were groundless. The worldly Henry of Bergen took
pity on the brooding cleric who had been temporarily assigned to
routine duties, and assured his deliverance by eventually sending
him off to France for advanced study in theology. Filled with enthusiasm, Erasmus enrolled at Montaigu College within the august
University of Paris in 1495.

Like graduate students everywhere, Erasmus found his living
conditions unbearable at Montaigu and sought relief by offering
vivid and unsolicited descriptions of his surroundings to sympathetic but powerless correspondents. His health soon deteriorated.
Racked by pain and subject to fainting spells, he was forced to
return to the Netherlands for a period of recuperation.[7] Who could

have foreseen such disaster? But his demoralizing confinement did
not endure. When forced to choose between Steyn with its mori-
bund silence and self-effacing monks and Paris with an inex-
haustible supply of books and inspiration, Erasmus spontaneously
regained his health and set out again for Paris. This time, however,
he took up residence outside the cloisters of Montaigu. He rented
a nearby flat so he could rest when he chose, eat whatever and
whenever he liked, and study late into the night, unencumbered
by custom and stifling protocol. At long last, Erasmus almost began to enjoy the academic life of the university. He now concentrated on questions of scholastic theology and language without
having to endure the austerity of the university's residence halls.
Poverty, however, soon restricted his earlier enthusiasm. Short of
funds, he found it necessary to tutor young men in Latin grammar
and rhetoric. As a tutor, Erasmus began to experiment with educational methods. He devised a number of textbooks which he
hoped would stimulate learning among his students. The most
famous of these popular texts is the delightful collection of dialogues entitled the *Colloquies,* some of which were written at this
time but not published until much later. Other works in this peda-
gogical series dealt with exposition and matters of curriculum.[8]
Moreover, mindful of the economic advantages which might ac-
crue, he preferred to teach only the affluent. It was in this way that
Erasmus struck up a lifelong friendship with the English nobleman
William Blount. What wisdom there was in his selection of that
particular student! For Blount fell almost immediately in awe of
the gifted teacher and soon extended an invitation to him to visit
England. By 1497 Erasmus had acquired a distaste for his Pa-
risian colleagues and the formal methods of scholastic instruction
which they promoted. He, therefore, looked forward to an opportunity to set aside his studies and to escape from the restrictive
atmosphere of Paris.[9] Thus, before the fifteenth century drew its
last breath, Erasmus settled at Oxford where he met such notables
as John Colet, later dean of St. Paul's, William Grocyn, and
Thomas Linacre, two eminent classical scholars, and the gifted
London barrister Thomas More.

   The turn of the century added a new dimension to Erasmus's
life. He became a cosmopolite—a citizen of the world.[10] Indeed,
throughout the first decade of the sixteenth century Erasmus was
on an almost continuous journey. He traveled in France, Italy,

and the Low Countries, forming friendships with the leading humanists of the age and promoting his own special interest in educational reform. During the course of his travels Erasmus published the earliest version of the *Enchiridion* or *Handbook of the Christian Soldier*. Addressed to the layman, this guide to moral behavior first appeared in 1503 and sketches Erasmus's concept of the philosophy of Christ. He encourages the sixteenth-century Christian to cultivate those virtues which are in keeping with the spirit of the gospel. By so doing, the individual strengthens his will and fortifies himself against the temptation to sin.

Moreover, in these formative years Erasmus acquired an appreciation of exegesis and intensified his study of Greek. He soon mastered the critical method of Valla and sought to apply the rigorous philological standards of this Italian humanist to biblical and patristic literature. Following the publication of Valla's *Annotations on the New Testament* in 1505, Erasmus issued Latin editions of numerous Greek authors, including Lucian, Euripides, and Plutarch.[11] In addition, Erasmus continued his formal studies and accepted a doctorate in theology from the University of Turin. While in Italy he also formed a profitable association with Aldus Manutius, the scholar-printer. Many of Erasmus's earliest works were to be issued by this Venetian: an enlarged edition of the *Adages* and new editions of Seneca, Plautus, and Terence are but four examples.[12]

With the appearance of the second edition of the *Adages* in 1508, Erasmus became the most celebrated teacher and promoter of humanism in Renaissance Europe.[13] At thirty-nine he was regarded by contemporary literati as the Prince of Humanists. They admired him for his erudition and sagacity and especially for his ability to write elegant Latin compositions. Indeed, nothing was more dearly prized in the sixteenth century than a holograph by Erasmus, and it is to his praise that Erasmus frequently employed the pen to write letters encouraging young, aspiring minds to adopt humanism and to cultivate intellectual tastes. His correspondence, which includes some two thousand surviving items,[14] brought the humanists of Europe together. Acknowledging Erasmus as its leader, the movement drew its strength and vitality from the Latin prose of this Dutch savant.

But by 1509 Erasmus had developed an aversion to traveling. The peripatetic inquirer now longed for the security of a permanent position. Encouraged by Henry VIII's ascension to the English throne and by the urgings of a former student, Lord Mountjoy, it is no surprise, therefore, that Erasmus returned to England; and through the influence of More, Archbishop William Warham, and Bishop John Fisher, he in 1511 was appointed Lady Margaret Professor of Divinity at Cambridge and a lecturer of Greek.[15] While en route from Italy to London, Erasmus devoted the idle hours to composing an early draft of his best remembered work, *In Praise of Folly.* Generally regarded as a literary masterpiece, this biting satire was written in the form of an extended declamation. The principal speaker, Folly, embodies the author's conception of human nature. As a humanist, Erasmus believed in man's innate goodness, but he also acknowledged man's predisposition to evil, suggesting that human error and transgression were frequently due to an imperfect understanding of God's law. Erasmus focuses attention on this concept of human nature in the course of his book. "You would never believe," Folly argues, "what sport and entertainment your mortal manikins provide daily for the gods. These gods, you know, set aside their sober forenoon hours for composing quarrels and giving ear to prayers. But after that, when they seek out some promontory of heaven and, setting there with faces bent downward, they watch what mortal men are adoring. There is no show like it. Good God, what a theater! How various the action of fools! . . . Here is a fellow dying for love of a sweet young thing, and the less he is loved in return the more helplessly he is in love. . . . Here is a man in mourning, but mercy me, what fool things he says and does! Hiring mourners as if they were actors, to play a comedy of grief!"[16]

In the sweeping satire that followed, Erasmus criticizes man's indulgence in self-love, laziness, sensuality, and intemperance. Society manages to go on day after day believing that its very existence somehow depends on perpetuating these vices. Erasmus holds all men responsible for this deplorable state of sixteenth-century society, but he reserves the sharpest satire for the academicians, monks, and those "scientists, reverenced for their beards and the fur on their gowns, who teach that they alone are wise while the rest of mortal men flit about as shadows. How pleasantly they dote, indeed, while they construct their numberless worlds, and measure the sun, moon, stars, and spheres as with thumb and line. They assign causes for lightning, winds, eclipses, and other inexplicable things, never hesitating a whit, as if they were privy to the secrets of nature, artificer of things, or as if they visited us fresh from the council of the gods. Yet all the while nature is laughing grandly at them and their conjectures." [17] Underlying the severity of his criticism, Erasmus reveals extraordinary compassion. He possessed both a humanitarian spirit and an instinct for social reform. He directed his attention to corruption wherever it might be detected: in the church, government, the family, the university. As Erasmus perceived it, institutional decay was simply a manifestation of a general disorientation. Sixteenth-century society was caught up in the selfish pursuit of pleasure because it had lost sight of perspective. Failing to understand the purpose of human existence, man was foolishly pursuing vanity and vice instead of perfecting human nature. But he did not despair. Drawing upon an earlier expression of faith in man, Erasmus saw a solution to man's dilemma in the adoption of a new Christian philosophy—a way of life based on virtue and love. If only man would imitate Jesus Christ. If only he would replace moral depravity with integrity of character and selfishness with sacrifice, mankind would begin an unparalleled upward ascent. Since society possessed the capacity to improve itself, all that was needed was an emphasis on humanity and a deemphasis on individual gratification. And what better way to restore human society than by recovering Christian unity. Indeed, the restoration of *Christiana Respublica* loomed always in the background of this reformer's mind.

For nearly three years, Erasmus remained at Cambridge. He enjoyed the English countryside and was inspired by the enthusiasm and goodwill of English humanists. In partial appreciation for all that had been given to him, he dedicated a textbook in 1512 to his friend and admirer John Colet, who had only recently refounded London's St. Paul's School.[18] Conceived as a thesaurus, *On Copia of Words and Ideas* is a collection of Latin phrases and idioms, culled from the classics, which offered the Renaissance learner an opportunity to enrich and enlarge his vocabulary. But even in the face of all this activity, he still felt incomplete. Perceiving the need for critical editions of the New Testament and the works of St. Jerome, Erasmus supervised the publication of these works at the press of Johann Froben in Basel. Although many printed versions of the New Testament were circulating in Europe at this time, there had been no inexpensive edition available to the educated bourgeoisie. Erasmus, therefore, filled an immensely important vacuum in 1516 when he completed a Greek version of the New Testament. It included both 'the Greek text and a Latin translation as well. As Margaret Mann Phillips has recorded: "Erasmus's greatest contribution to his time [now] lay before the world."[19] *The Novum Instrumentum* had a revolutionary effect on biblical exegesis. Not only did Martin Luther consult it in preparing his translation of the New Testament but the work itself contributed to a general movement espousing Church reform and a return to early Christianity. Erasmus enjoyed this period of respite. He loved scholarship and the smell of printer's ink! But restlessness soon gripped him once more. Yearning to travel, he returned to Holland and Germany, and even managed trips to England in 1515 and 1517.

Shortly after his third trip to England, Erasmus produced the *Education of a Christian Prince* (1516). In this work he suggests that the purpose of government is to secure the advancement of human society rather than to promote the selfish ambitions of individual princes. This humanitarian and moralistic orientation offers sharp contrast to the statecraft of Machiavelli's *Il Principe.* Erasmus also promoted the idea of man's educability, and ultimately preferred an elective system of monarchy to a hereditary one.[20] But Erasmus himself was a supranationalist. He grew to distrust nationalism and equated patriotism with chauvinism. In an effort to reform society, he wanted to instruct ecclesiastical and secular leaders in how to govern wisely and to instill in them the importance of acquiring peaceful methods of persuasion. Above all, he wanted them to rely more on arbitration than on weapons of war. Erasmus expressed his deep concern for peace in a second treatise, entitled *The Complaint of Peace* (1517). An avowed pacifist, the Prince of Humanists condemned warfare in general and suggested some practical ways on how to avoid future wars. The moral tone of Erasmus's two political treatises served as an introduction to one of the truly great classics of the Renaissance, the *Colloquies.* First published in 1518, these pungent dialogues were, as we have indicated, originally intended as a handbook to learning Latin, but their combined impact was considerably greater. They offered the inquiring student both a running commentary on contemporary events and an exposé on social, political, and religious corruption. Erasmus's wit and common sense appealed especially to the middle class, which now stuffed its conversation with quotations from the *Colloquies* and soon entered the arena of humanistic debate. Combining travel and scholarship, Erasmus roamed about the Low Countries for seven years in search of men and ideas. But at last the wandering ceased. It was now time to set in print the many thoughts which had occupied him during the past two decades. With this in mind, he accepted an invitation from Froben and took up residence in Basel. Here from 1521 to 1529, he acted as the general editor of Froben's press and produced a steady stream of religious tracts. Certainly, the most important of these publications is the one which was directed to Martin Luther. Entitled *Discourse on Free Will,* this calm restatement of scholastic theology grew out of a heated exchange of letters between the "Wittenberg gladiator" and his supporters.[21] By 1524 Erasmus and Luther had adopted such entrenched positions that no amount of sagacity or correspondence could resolve their differences. And something of the width and depth of that growing chasm is revealed in Erasmus's treatise on free will. Since errors in judgment may be caused by man's intellectual limitations, Erasmus cautioned Luther against accepting with certitude matters of an interpretive nature. Only clearly revealed truths can be accepted unconditionally.

As a reformer, Erasmus was a moderate. He generally preferred compromise and scholarly dialogue to revolt and public debate. Through his philosophy of Christ, he envisioned a new world committed to the exercise of Christian virtue and individual responsibility. At the same time, he tried to restore primitive Christianity and to encourage inward spirituality. Erasmus's concept of Christian piety was offended by weekend pilgrimages and public processions. Such hollow displays of religious fervor seemed hopelessly out of step with the image of the historical Jesus. Pleading for more belief but fewer beliefs, he was willing to trim down the Credo in favor of a limited number of basic truths. Since Christ represented the best of all models, and his life had been dedicated to interior holiness and public service, the sixteenth century, and centuries to come, would do well to imitate him.

At the height of his career, such eminent artists as Albrecht Dürer, Hans Holbein the Younger, and Quentin Metsys recorded for posterity the engaging profile of Desiderius Erasmus.[22] All these artists exhibit much in common, but of the many portraits of Erasmus which have been produced, the most compelling one is by Metsys. Completed in 1517, this extraordinary painting hangs in the Corsini Gallery in Rome. The subject appears recollected, clothed in the *vestimentum clausum* of the cleric-academician. Lined with fur, his outer cloak appears almost luxurious on close examination. A gold ring, which is worn on the right index finger, accentuates this quality and acknowledges his doctor of divinity status. The head of Erasmus, wearing a doctoral cap, is seen in three-quarter view, turned slightly to the viewer's left. Attached to his waist is a black purse, conspicuous for its gold trim.

Standing in front of an open book, Erasmus rests his left hand on a page of this unidentified tome and, with his other hand, composes an inscription on the opposite leaf. The room in which he is working is starkly simple. Even the subdued colors of the painting, mostly browns and oranges, emphasize the introspective pose of the subject. But the focal point of Metsys's portrait is the haunting visage of the scholar and bibliophile. Our eyes are immediately drawn to his dignified and delicate features. Stamped with mental acuity, the face is both serene and infectious. Yet it is the downcast eyes, those small, dark, penetrating beacons of lights which somehow add depth and intensity to his thin and pale countenance. The high cheek bones, angular nose, and pursed lips, on the other hand, make him appear almost dour. But even in this gloomy setting, his silent looks and carriage betray an inward feeling: Erasmus loved humanity.

Although this portrait and those by Holbein and Dürer may convey the impression that Erasmus was an icy and sober introvert, who was immersed in his scholarship and in himself, such was not the case. Far from being shy or reserved, Erasmus possessed an extraordinary ability to make friends, and this gregarious side of his personality gives abundant testimony to a warm and compassionate disposition. He loved many men deeply and frequently expressed his affection by years of faithful correspondence. The names of James Batt, Thomas More, Boniface Amerbach, Peter Gilles, and Beatus Rhenanus are but a few respresentative examples of persons who reciprocated Erasmus's comradeship with pride and gravity.[23]

In these letters and in his major publications Erasmus wrote with both flexibility and grace; and, yet, very little of what he wrote can be classified as purely literary. Except for a few poems, all of his writing had a very practical purpose: problems of morality or social and political questions were uppermost in his mind. And no matter what point of view or position he assumed in his various works, Erasmus's faith remained unshaken. For him it was the interior life of grace that really mattered. Fortified with unswerving confidence, he was able to launch his testy barbs and to withstand the expected but explosive reactions. Erasmus was truly the archetype of the sixteenth-century intellectual. Although born in embarrassing obscurity, he rose to undisputed heights by means of his publications.

1524 was the watershed of Erasmus's career. To maintain his independence, Erasmus declined the gifts of popes and princes, avoided royal courts and lived in Switzerland, far away from the Netherlands, France, England, Italy, and Germany where he had lived so fully in the past and had earned so many honors and so much praise. Despite his self-imposed exile, however, he lived to see his works condemned, his disciples dispersed, and his dreams unfulfilled. Erasmus was torn between two extremes. For his refusal to support Luther and the cause of Protestant reform he has been condemned as a coward. But his refusal to take sides, his refusal to join either camp, was a mark of courage and dedication to principle. There was no temerity in his silence. Even though Erasmus sympathized with Luther's criticism and saw the need for reform, he did not think that Luther offered a better alternative. Erasmus was committed to Christendom. Above all, he wished to preserve the unity of an institutional Church—a church founded by Christ and protected by the Holy Spirit. Hating war, he saw a solution to the vexing choice between compromise or revolt in the *Philosophia Christi*. Though at times, Erasmus was caught between principle and practicality, and was buffeted by indecision and by forces and events beyond prophecy and control, he never lost sight of his goal. With reassuring élan, he condemned fanaticism, dogmatism, and pride, upheld personal independence, applauded compromise, and sought to unite mankind.

After eight years in Basel, Erasmus was forced to leave. The city which had offered him a haven for nearly a decade now closed its mind and accepted the intolerance of a radical reformation.[24] Beginning in 1529, he lived in Freiburg, during which time the city fathers and the university showered him with honors. But somehow, his vitality had been sapped. Europe was then at war and he saw his life-struggle for universal brotherhood and human progress degenerate into mindless chaos. Even England with its circle of brilliant humanists had given itself over to fratricide. What comfort was there now in thinking about England's future when that country's barbaric king had taken the lives of two of mankind's most humane personalities, Sir Thomas More and the saintly bishop of Rochester, John Fisher? [25]

Something of Erasmus's dolefulness and despondency can be detected in a series of later portraits. Hans Holbein, especially, succeeds in revealing a sense of abject resignation and a public expression of failure. This artist's 1531 portrait of Erasmus is a great deal different from the relatively flattering image produced by Metsys in 1517. And, indeed, Erasmus had changed during the fifteen years which separated the two paintings. By the middle of the thirties, he was filled with uncontrollable ennui. Bent toward death, the withering sage almost pleaded for his deliverance. Only the grave could spare him from further unpleasantness and disappointment. What a relief it would be to rejoin those departed friends who had been snuffed out by intolerance and inhumanity. Apparently sensing Erasmus's melancholy, Holbein preserved it on canvas in an oval-shaped portrait which can be found in the print room of the Öffentliche Kunstsammlung in Basel. Now that he had grown gray, now that his strength had begun to diminish, Erasmus stands helpless, imprisoned within an oval frame. He appears disillusioned, gaunt, and ailing. Even the cruel scars of old age have by this time parched his tired face. During the past forty years, Erasmus had spent a life dedicated to scholarship and human welfare, but in proceeding along this lonely path, it finally became clear to him that he had, at last, reached an impasse. A scholar to the very end of his life, Erasmus, nevertheless, made a final visit to Basel in 1535 in order to edit the works of Origen. While at work on this new edition, he died at the age of sixty-six in the home of Jerome Froben, the son of his old friend. Death found him as it had found his great Italian precursor, Petrarch, in study and in prayer.

Erasmus of Rotterdam is a unique example among Renaissance writers of an intellectual whose earthly role was essentially public, but whose everyday life was primarily withdrawn. Somehow, Erasmus found strength for his public responsibilities in the hidden life of a scholarly recluse. And, yet, without that incomparable face and ethereal voice, Erasmus on the printed page was never to inspire in later generations what the magnetism of his personal presence had created in his own day. Erasmus, as a subtle critic, was face to face a living myth—the appointed leader of a generation who arrives at the beginning of a new age, sounds a collective hope and purpose, and before fading into the background conveys spiritual strength to others.

The greatness of Erasmus, however, lies in the conviction that truth, spoken with love and patience, if not wit and grace, is a more potent instrument of reform than force or invective. Trusting always in the love of God, Erasmus believed that every man could promote human progress by becoming an imitator of Christ and an inheritor of heaven. In his learning and candor, Erasmus is without equal in the Northern Renaissance. Behind every faint smile and twinkling eyelid there is both brilliance and clarity of expression. As a writer, he is among that small group of elite men who succeed in winning our admiration and affection. Erasmus also impresses us with his rare critical powers and intuitions. We might well join him in deploring the dichotomy existing between pure thought and experience and the lack of critical scholarship which leads to a heavy dependence on authority. The spontaneity, vigor, and independence of mind which characterize this complex man emerge from even the most casual reading of the record. Highly critical of formalism and bureaucracy, Erasmus sought truth in the word of the gospel. He also sought personal freedom, not through revolt or isolation, but through involvement. And he ended his life in the conviction that the way he lived was in imitation of Christ.

Erasmus's life was private and was lived simply. Since he looked upon political institutions as a threat to his security as well as an affront to his faith in Christianity, he jealously guarded his own personal freedom. In living, he sought few acquisitions. He prized love and morality above all else. And, although the satisfaction which he sought through love could not be fully realized in his own lifetime, he was able to create a life of partial fulfillment by writing. Indeed, writing was his one great instrument of reform. By means of his pen he produced a pulsating prose that always took the form of personal experience. His rapier wit and laconic style made even the shortest of his colloquies worth more than a hundred syllogisms. The admiring reader cannot help but respond to the compelling emotion in his pages—his impatience with authority, his natural vagabondage, his ability to remain true to his soul and to the social world about him. This sense of commitment is what is most vital and vivid in the man and his work. Erasmus lived a full life of the mind and knew how to share his hidden thoughts. He knew the value of joy. And those who were close to him knew it too.

Erasmus the Hum

By JAMES D. TRACY

James D. Tracy, Assistant Professor of History at the University of Minnesota, is a graduate of St. Louis University, Johns Hopkins University, the University of Notre Dame, and Princeton University. While a graduate student at the above institutions, he held a Danforth fellowship. Dr. Tracy began his teaching career at the University of Michigan before accepting a position at the University of Minnesota. In addition to the article which appeared in the Fall, 1968, issue of the *Renaissance Quarterly* entitled "Erasmus Becomes a German," he has contributed to the *Bibliothèque d'Humanisme et Renaissance* and devoted his Princeton dissertation ("Erasmus: The Growth of a Mind") to Erasmus's intellectual development.

Humanism is commonly thought to be the philosophy of the Renaissance, a new appreciation of human dignity and freedom in contrast to the medieval emphasis on authority and on the miseries of this earthly life. The humanism of Erasmus has sometimes been defined in this way. Gerhard Ritter finds the essence of Renaissance humanism in Erasmus's defense of free will: the famous controversy with Luther proves that the man-centered philosophy of humanism was not compatible with the God-centered theology of the Reformation.[1] But Lorenzo Valla, a fifteenth-century Italian humanist whom Erasmus admired, wrote a treatise against the freedom of the will which was cited by Luther.[2] Younger humanists in Germany during Erasmus's lifetime were not aware of any incompatibility between humanism and Reformation theology, for most of them became Protestants.[3] Erasmus himself was an original thinker in some areas but not in philosophy. When compelled to write against Luther he did choose the subject of free will. But he borrowed his arguments from the third-century theologian Origen and from St. Thomas Aquinas.[4] If his n depended solely on the treatise *Concerning Free Choice* uld long since have been forgotten. Thus the humanism of a, the young Germans, and Erasmus must have been something other than a philosophy.

There was no single philosophical doctrine on which all humanists agreed. The one thing which almost all of them did have in common was a love of classical Latin. Their fascination with Latin style seems strange to modern readers; historians often ignore it and concentrate on other facets of humanism more interesting to the twentieth century. But Paul O. Kristeller, the leading contemporary student of humanism, rightly insists that a definition of humanism must begin with what humanists had most in common. They insisted that classical Latin style was useful as well as beautiful. In fourteenth-century Italy, where humanism arose, there was great demand for men who could speak and write Latin effectively. Francesco Petrarca, the father of humanism, popularized the idea that Cicero was the best model for a persuasive and eloquent style.[5] Some humanists analyzed the techniques of persuasion employed by Cicero. Others studied the properties of vocabulary and syntax by which classical Latin differed from medieval Latin. Thus a preoccupation with classical style led to a cultivation of rhetoric and grammar. These two disciplines constituted the core of the intellectual interests shared by most humanists. It will be necessary to explore the implications of each before the humanism of Erasmus can be properly described.

Rhetoric in ancient Athens was the great rival of philosophy. Socrates the philosopher charged that students who went to the teachers of rhetoric learned only the art of winning arguments by trickery, not the art of reasoning in search of truth. Teachers of rhetoric retorted that students who went to Socrates wasted their time chewing over insoluble questions. The art of rhetoric, however, would be useful and profitable in the law courts and public assemblies. It would also promote virtuous habits, for no one could be a successful orator unless he were known to be a man of good character.[6] Plato continued Socrates' criticisms of rhetoric. But as Greek culture was transmitted to the west the philosophers had no true successors among the practical-minded Romans. The two great Latin writers on education took over the theory and practice of Greek rhetoric. Quintilian's *Institutes of Oratory* laid down general principles of educational method as well as principles of effective speaking. Cicero suggested that the orator should gain a broad knowledge of human nature through what he called the *studia humanitatis* or the humanities: poetry, history, and moral philosophy.[7] To be a successful orator one also had to be virtuous: for it was the orator's noble duty to persuade his fellow citizens to follow the path of reason, just as in past ages the power of eloquence had persuaded savage men to descend from their caves and dwell together in cities.[8] In his treatises on philosophy Cicero was less interested in what might be true in theory than in what was conducive to morality.[9] The purpose of education was not to indulge the mind in speculation but to train good citizens. Renaissance humanism was a revival of Cicero's educational program, just as medieval scholasticism had been a revival of Aristotelian philosophy. The main undergraduate subjects in medieval universities had been the logic and physics of Aristotle. Only in the fourteenth century did the subjects recommended by Cicero begin to be taught in Italian universities. A teacher of poetry was known in student slang as an *umanista*—a humanist. Humanists and teachers of logic sometimes debated the nature of education in terms that resembled the ancient debate between rhetoricians and philosophers. Thus Professor Kristeller concludes that humanism was a phase in the rhetorical tradition of Western culture.[10]

Rhetoric was an art of speaking which claimed to promote civic virtue. The argument which Cicero and Quintilian used to support this claim is important for an understanding of humanism. They began with the premise, borrowed from Stoic philosophy, that "seeds" of goodness—a natural inclination to virtue—were implanted in the human spirit.[11] Men were endowed not only with reason but also with a sense of honor, which Plato had said was reason's natural ally in the struggle against base desires. The passion for honor could be dangerous if not controlled but Cicero pointed out that a sense of compassion or *humanitas* was also a part of human nature.[12] Thus men had an inborn sense of right and wrong just as they had an inborn sense of what was noble and beautiful. Abstract speculation about the nature of justice might make the mind more agile but it did not make men more virtuous. Men were ready to follow the path of virtue if only they could be persuaded; this was the task of the orator. A free man would resist whatever might be imposed on him by force but it was in keeping with his dignity to be persuaded. Quintilian applied these ideas to education. Learning was retarded when a teacher applied harsh punishment, promoted when he appealed to the ambition of his pupils.[13] Thus in defense of their craft the Latin rhetoricians developed a pragmatic suspicion of theoretical philosophy and an optimistic belief in the moral improvement of men by means of persuasion and education.

Renaissance humanists adopted the rationale of classical rhetoric as well as its techniques. Jerrold Seigel has shown that the Italian humanists of the fourteenth and fifteenth century sought to carry out Cicero's plan of subordinating philosophy to the practical needs of persuasion. Northern humanists developed a theory of consensus, according to which truth in ethics was founded not on logical arguments but on assumptions shared by all men, which the ancient rhetoricians had called "commonplaces."[14] Humanist educators agreed with Cicero that men had a natural desire to learn. They recommended appealing to a pupil's sense of pride instead of using physical punishment.[15] It may seem at this point that the discussion is returning to its beginning. The philosophical assumptions shared by humanists and rhetoricians sound like the emphasis on human freedom and dignity that was supposed to be an inadequate definition of humanism. The difference is a matter of context. During a certain period of history men who shared certain intellectual interests were called "humanists" by their contemporaries. If humanism becomes a naked idea, lifted from context, it becomes difficult to explain why the humanists were usually suspicious of speculative philosophy, or why Thomas Aquinas was not a humanist. Conversely, the context makes it easier to understand the aristocratic attitudes of the humanists. Cicero and Quintilian shared the common assumption of most ancient writers that the capacity for virtue was found primarily if not exclusively among members of the upper classes. The humanists, who often moved among the chief men of their society, had a higher opinion than ancient writers did of merchants but not of the lower classes. Finally, apart from the context it would be tempting to contrast humanist optimism about human nature with the pessimism of St. Augustine or Thomas Hobbes. In fact such a contrast would be misleading because the humanists, particularly in northern Europe, were primarily educators. Like their favorite classical authors they were concerned with moral ideals and not with the realities of power. They believed that an atmosphere of freedom was fitting for aristocrats and learned men. But no more than Hobbes or Augustine would they have welcomed the idea of extending such freedom to the common crowd of men. Rational persuasion was for the few and not for the masses.

The art of rhetoric alone was not sufficient to revive the eloquence of the ancients. The art of grammar was required to overcome the differences that separated the spoken Latin of the Church and the universities from the Latin of Cicero. Humanists were outraged that medieval writers had departed from the classical norm in vocabulary, sentence structure, and the rules of versification. Lorenzo Valla's *Elegantiae* or *Book of Elegances* sought to counteract ten centuries of linguistic change. The Latin tongue was "a great mystery, indeed a divine power." But the Gothic tribes who destroyed the empire of the Romans had also devastated their language. Classical purity was to be restored through Valla's collection of over three thousand "elegances" or illustrations of correct usage.[16] Humanists divided the history of language into three stages of perfection, degeneration, and revival, thus anticipating the eighteenth-century division of European history into ancient, medieval, and renaissance periods. They themselves expanded their criticism of medieval Latin culture into other areas besides linguistic usage. Classical authors had to be reinterpreted because of misunderstandings that arose from the medieval emphasis on dialectic. The corpus of an author's works had to be purged not only of copyists' errors but also of spurious works that had been naively accepted by medieval readers. The science of philology or textual criticism became a vehicle for exposing the false historical basis of many cherished medieval beliefs. For example, the so-called *Donation of Constantine,* a purportedly contemporary account of how the Emperor Constantine "donated" the western half of his empire to a Pope who had cured him of leprosy had been used by medieval popes to support their territorial claims. Lorenzo Valla was not the first to doubt its authenticity, but he was the first to show on the basis of linguistic evidence that it could not have been written as early as the fourth century. Valla also proved in controversy with a Franciscan friar that the Apostles' Creed was not written by the Apostles. More importantly, he initiated textual study of the Greek New Testament.[17] In this way the humanist preoccupation with elegant style developed toward a new critical understanding of history. Philology was to be humanism's most solid contribution to the intellectual heritage of Europe.

In order to imitate classical Latin the humanists cultivated the arts of rhetoric and grammar. Rhetoric implied a utilitarian attitude toward philosophy and an optimistic theory of education. Grammar led to the emergence of a new sense of the past. Long ago Richard McKeon suggested that the differences between humanism and scholasticism might be explained by the differing intellectual methods of grammar and rhetoric as opposed to logic or dialectic.[18] This definition of humanism too is open to criticism but it does have the advantage that it fits Erasmus. Erasmus was not just a humanist. He learned much from the Fathers of the Church, and possibly also from the religious milieu in which he was raised, as well as from the classics. His ideas stem not just from reading but also from contemporary life, from friends, and from his own personality. In a fuller study of Erasmus these other strands would also have to be followed. But he was clearly a humanist in his love of classical Latin, his hopes for the moral improvement of mankind through education, and his great contribution to the science of philology. In his writings these humanist concerns merge into a new program for the reform of European society based on reforms in education and religion. Erasmus the humanist can best be understood as Erasmus the humanist reformer. The discussion will take up first his humanist philosophy of education and second his humanist theology.

*   *   *

Letters dating from Erasmus's teen-age years show that he was already an admirer of the classics. His first literary work was a digest of Lorenzo Valla's *Book of Elegances*. Shortly before or afterwards he entered the monastery of Augustinian Canons near the Dutch city of Gouda. Soon he was persuading other young monks to share his literary enthusiasms, especially Horace. Like many humanists he was not content unless his intellectual pleasure had some ethical justification. He told his friends that through the study of poetry they would become more honest and charitable in their dealings with others.[19] Older monks were probably skeptical about the value of pagan authors. Erasmus called them morose and complained of being ridiculed and restricted in his freedom.

Opposition real or imagined converted his love of the classics into a campaign against the enemies of good literature. *The Book against the Barbarians,* his first major work, was begun in 1489 and revised in 1494. By this time he had "escaped" from the monastery. The Bishop of Cambrai needed someone fluent in Latin since he expected to be called to Rome for a cardinal's hat. Erasmus was recommended and gladly accepted. When the trip failed to materialize the Bishop gave him money to study at the University of Paris.[20] In Paris, between 1495 and 1499, he supplemented his pension by taking in pupils. As a tutor he attempted to replace the old schoolbooks with new texts that would teach classical Latin. His most successful efforts were a treatise *De Copia, On the Fullness of Style,* and a collection of *Adages* or sayings of the ancients.[21] Thus for ten years Erasmus was preoccupied with the humanist dream of a new and better education. In his early works, and in later works devoted to education,[22] he was concerned first to show the failings of the prevailing system of education, and second to justify a new kind of education based on the classics. These two aspects of his humanist pedagogy, negative and positive, can be considered each in turn.

He attacked the primary or secondary education of his day on three familiar points: the teachers were brutal, the books were full of barbarisms, and the whole curriculum, even prior to entrance in the universities, was oriented around dialectic. Schoolteachers in the Middle Ages had a reputation for thrashing their pupils regularly. German slang terms for teacher seem to focus on this part of the pedagogue's profession: one was "Arschpauker," or "ass-drummer."[23] Like other humanists Erasmus had a story of how he himself had for a time lost interest in learning because of a teacher's brutality.[24] He followed Valla in his criticism of medieval Latin books. They were particularly bad because of farfetched etymologies and word associations. For example, part of the definition of the word "dog" was that a dog "adheres." This was so because of the gospel passage in which dogs are said to return to their own vomit. According to theologians the "dogs" in question were heretics who returned to their own false doctrines. The word "heretic" (which was actually Greek) was thought to derive from the Latin "adhaereo" or "adhere." Therefore dogs, like heretics, "adhere." After laboring through arguments of this kind one might better appreciate the sense of liberation that humanists ex-

perienced with classical Latin.[25] Finally, Erasmus felt much harm
had come from the permeation of lower schools by dialectic. As
taught in the universities, dialectic produced more arrogance than
learning. Its introduction into lower schools meant that Latin
grammars, instead of simply describing usage, attempted to derive
usage from a set of axioms. Schoolboys thus had to wrestle with
logic before properly learning to read and write.[26]

Thus far Erasmus's attack on medieval education contains nothing that cannot be found in humanists like Valla or, as regards the
arrogance of dialecticians, in reform-minded churchmen as well.
His expectation that men trained in scholasticism would be vain
and quarrelsome was simply an application of the basic humanist
belief that a man's character could be molded by education.[27] He
did, however, articulate the details of the argument more fully than
others. Latin was learned by memorizing definitions and following
strict rules. Teachers stood ready with a cane to ensure, for
example, that a composition contained just so many lines and no
more.[28] At the university the same students learned in the study
of dialectic to concentrate all their mental powers on each fine
point of an opponent's argument. Unlike other humanists Erasmus
saw little positive value in the study of dialectic.[29] He seems to
have felt that both dialectic and the rigid discipline of the schools
constricted the energies of students within narrow channels and
trained them to find their pleasure or satisfaction in attacking
others; both would be illustrations of the humanist premise, found
especially in Quintilian, that students are made bitter and rebel-
lious by excessive constraint. Whatever his reasoning, he clearly
did believe that the current system of education was responsible
for producing theologians who spent their days hunting for heresies instead of studying the scriptures, and preachers who, instead
of instructing the people, fulminated in righteous anger against
married priests.[30]

Erasmus's positive argument for classical education was likewise a new articulation of common humanist assumptions. Somewhat more than Cicero he identified "seeds of virtue" in human
nature with the gentle instincts of peace and concord.[31] These
qualities would be fostered by the studies recommended by Cicero
and the educational methods recommended by Quintilian. Erasmus believed that a humane character could be formed not only
by the study of good literature but also by the imitation of classical

style. A student who practiced speaking and writing in the clear, harmonious style of the ancients, and who steeped himself daily in the elegant wisdom of Cicero or Horace, could not fail to grow in dignity and compassion. The argument was similar to Plato's contention that simple and harmonious music would foster a noble character, except that Erasmus, who had little to say for music, was a great lover of words.[32] He presumed that students would be eager to learn. Hence they had more need of encouragement than of discipline. The ideal tutor would be a personal friend to his pupils. He would discern each one's peculiar talent. He would not prescribe too many rules and would make learning a game rather than a chore. All of these ideas were in Quintilian.[33] But Erasmus was not just a disciple. Quintilian had discouraged the use of extemporaneous composition as an exercise; the serious business of the law courts demanded careful preparation. Italian humanist educators of the fifteenth century echoed Quintilian on this point.[34] Erasmus was less interested in forensic language than in ordinary conversation. He knew that students of his day required special practice in order to converse freely in a language that was not their native tongue. He also had a theory about the connection between language habits and character formation. Thus he encouraged friends to practice writing extemporaneously on the grounds that it would train them to be more candid.[35] Even more than Quintilian he believed in relaxing the rules and inhibitions of traditional education. The new education that he envisioned would be a mirror image of the prevailing system. An education which concentrated on dialectic and depended on the fear of punishment produced men of a violent and aggressive temperament. An education focussed on the humanities and depending on a free self-expression would produce men of a generous and peace-loving temperament. Thus Erasmus argued, as other humanists had before him, that reforms in the classroom would make students into better citizens.[36]

He continued to produce books that could be used for the new curriculum. His book of adages, which numbered 800 when first published in 1500, swelled to over 3,000 in the Venice edition of 1508. This was the book that made Erasmus famous. Humanist schoolmasters and their pupils were eager for just such a collection of nuggets of ancient wisdom. During his stay in Italy, from 1506 to 1509, he also composed several model orations to illustrate the principles of rhetoric.[37] But his real talent lay elsewhere. In 1501 he had published explanatory notes to Cicero's *De Officiis, On Moral Duties*. In 1504 he discovered a manuscript of Lorenzo Valla's notes to the Greek New Testament and brought it to Paris for publication.[38] He resolved to carry on Valla's textual work, not merely in the New Testament but with St. Jerome and Seneca and many other authors. For most of his adult life Erasmus would be primarily a philologist.

Meanwhile, in the decades between 1500 and 1520, humanism made steady advances in the town schools of Germany and the Low Countries. Erasmus became the great prophet of change in the curriculum that took place during his own lifetime. Humanist schoolmasters struggled bravely to make classical Latin the spoken language of a new generation. They could not foresee that the growth of national states would promote vernacular languages at the expense of Latin. In other ways too they failed to reach their objectives. In a careful study of Dutch Latin schools in the sixteenth century, P. N. M. Bot concludes that the much-vaunted humanist revolution produced in the end only minor changes. Students did have more exposure than before to classical literature, but their understanding of it was colored by pedantic and moralistic humanist commentaries. Humanist Latin grammars were sometimes longer and more cumbersome than the medieval texts they replaced. Schoolmasters continued to regard physical punishment as normal and necessary. Finally, as R. R. Bolgar points out in his study of the classical heritage, pupils in the second generation of humanist schools were given commentaries and digests to read and the classical authors were once more shunted aside.[39] The fact that humanist educational theory did not always work out as planned cannot be blamed entirely on the teachers. Educational theorists like Erasmus were, in Bot's phrase, rather cerebral. They lived quiet, orderly lives in which everything was supposed to have a rational purpose. They overlooked the fact that most schoolboys were not very much excited by classical literature. The humanist theory of education, like the ancient rhetorical theory of persuasion, was in a way aristocratic. Erasmus did recommend that boys attend a town school, whereas Quintilian had preferred a private tutor. But he wrote about what education should be like for boys who were as talented and eager to learn as he had been; he never taught in a classroom.[40] The classical curriculum designed by the humanists has by now largely disappeared; it is thought to be a relic of the days when only the sons of the upper classes were considered fit to be educated. But the theory behind the curriculum —a theory which runs from Quintilian through the humanists into modern times—continues to be taken seriously by those concerned with reforming a system of education whose assumptions are democratic.

*   *   *

Among his contemporaries Erasmus was even more famous as a religious reformer. At some point which is difficult to date his main interest shifted from classical literature to theology. He went to Paris in 1495 to study scholastic theology but while there was obviously more interested in the classics. John Colet in England and Jean le Voirier in Flanders pointed the way to a new theology based more on personal conviction and a study of the Bible. After meeting Colet in 1499 Erasmus took up the arduous task of learning Greek in order to study the New Testament.[41] But in 1503 he was apparently angling for a place at the court of Prince Philip of Burgundy.[42] In 1504 he promised Colet he would devote himself to the New Testament. But his years in Italy were spent on the *Adages* and other classical projects.[43] Finally, after a long and obscure stay in England from 1509 to 1514, he emerged with a vast store of learning in theology and church history. The fruition of these quiet years came in 1516 with the publication of his Greek New Testament and his edition of St. Jerome.[44] In 1503, when he published a treatise called the *Enchiridion* or *Handbook of the Militant Christian,* it attracted little attention. But a new edition of the same work in the German city of Strassburg in 1515 was a great success.[45] When it became known that the famous Erasmus had something to say about the reform of the church, the educated public, especially in Germany, was eager to listen. In theology as in education Erasmus developed humanist principles into an original program of reform. His theology was by no means entirely of humanist inspiration. But important humanist elements can be found first in his overwhelming emphasis on the moral or ethical dimension of religion, and second in his program for bringing about a reformation of morals.

Erasmus believed that religious reform was necessary because

"the morals of Christians" at the present time "are worse than
those of any age." Above all, the constant warfare among Christian states demonstrated that European society was not really
Christian. The Princes went to war for what Erasmus regarded as trivial
and unnecessary reasons; men on either side marched off without
hesitation to mutual slaughter.[46] Part of the difficulty lay in the
character of medieval religion. Christians paid too little attention
to the ethical teachings of the Gospel because they paid too much
attention to dogma. Like Cicero Erasmus was skeptical about the
value of speculative philosophy or speculative theology; the real
test of truth for any doctrine lay not in its logical coherence but
in its practical effects in the lives of men. Many so-called dogmas
were simply the opinions of theologians and had never been
accepted by the whole church: dogmas became established not
by the arguments of theologians, nor by the decrees of popes, but
by the consensus of believers over the centuries—just as, in the
writings of other humanists, the consensus of mankind was authori-
tative on moral questions.[47] Even in the case of dogmas that were
accepted by the universal church Erasmus gave some weight to
pragmatic considerations: the doctrine of free will should perhaps
not be preached because it encouraged human arrogance; the doctrine of the real presence of Christ in the Eucharist should perhaps
not be insisted on if it caused division among Christians. He found
nothing in the great fourth-century controversy over the divinity
of Christ to justify the harm that was done to Christian unity.
Personally he sympathized with the (Semi-) Arian party, which
had professed the divinity of Christ while refusing to say that He
was "consubstantial" with the Father. The Semi-Arians had lost
and the term "consubstantial" had become a part of orthodoxy.
Erasmus would not dispute the verdict of history but neither could
he find any sense in it.[48] He always spoke more of Jesus the moral
teacher than of Christ the Redeemer. Even within the sphere of
moral teaching he sometimes maintained that the New Testament
ethic was already present within the human spirit. He emphasized
not the doctrines peculiar to Christianity but the universal teachings
of peace and love. The celebration of mass in rival army camps
was true sacrilege; forced interpretations of Scripture to buttress
papal wars were "true heresies, true blasphemies against the most
sacred dogmas of Christ."[49]

For centuries scholars have debated whether or not Erasmus

in effect reduced the Christian religion to the status of being an ethic and nothing more. Augustin Renaudet, a French scholar who devoted a lifetime of research to Erasmus, concluded that he outwardly professed loyalty to the Catholic Church while inwardly he looked forward to the emergence of a new, ethical form of Christianity in which there would be no fixed or unchanging dogmas. Renaudet's critics point out, however, that the early Christian writers whom Erasmus studied, and writers in the tradition of late medieval piety in which he was educated, sometimes criticized a purely speculative theology and emphasized the moral requirements of religion just as strongly as he did.[50] At the other end of the spectrum of opinion, Ernst-Wilhelm Kohls, a young German scholar, has shown recently that Erasmus makes orthodox assertions of all the basic Christian dogmas even in his early writings, which are considered to be the most humanistic. But Kohls is too much the systematic or dialectical theologian: he is content to quote statements at face value without attempting to assess their meaning in context, or their weight relative to other assertions.[51] The question as to the relation between humanist ethics and Christian theology in the writings of Erasmus can never be resolved because its resolution would depend on theological presuppositions. Christian thought has always oscillated between an emphasis on God's immanent presence in the world and an emphasis on God's transcendence of all created things. Some theologians will assert that religion is distinct from ethics, others will deny it. Some will be angered by Erasmus's firm belief that moral conduct is the test of truth in matters of doctrine, others will rejoice.[52] To fix the range of orthodoxy within this field of tension is not a task for historians.

Erasmus was a humanist also in the structure of his program for the reformation of Christendom. His premises were that Christian people were made fearful and self-righteous by a false religion of external observances, that the words of the New Testament in its true meaning contained a marvelous power to change men's lives, and that the inner promptings of human nature itself were in sympathy with the message of the New Testament. He wrote the *Enchiridion* "in order to remedy the error of those who place all religion in the observance of certain more-than-Jewish ceremonies."[53] "Ceremonies" included any external religious acts that Christians were commanded to perform under pain of sin. Ceremonies had originated among Christians with monastic observances, but, since monks were considered to be the most perfect Christians, various obligations, such as abstaining from meat on Friday or attending mass on holy days, were gradually made universal by the church. Thus ceremonies had become "the plague of all Christendom." [54] The evil effects of a religion of ceremonies could still best be observed among those most burdened by ritual obligations. Having been taught that God would be angry if they so much as mispronounced a syllable in choir, monks lived in constant fear of trespassing on the rules that circumscribed their lives. The very fact that they performed so many obligations so scrupulously made them certain of being superior to ordinary Christians. Men devoted to the service of God should be cheerful and kind. But monks were "morose at table, scarcely tolerable even to themselves." This was because the regimen of ceremonies fostered "an envy more than womanish, 'a military wrath and ferocity, a never-satisfied lust for quarreling." [55] Laymen were threatened with the pains of hell if they ate meat on Fridays or worked in the fields on Sundays. Many of the clergy exploited popular ignorance by promoting observances in which they had a selfish interest. Clerical "tyranny" over laymen was most obvious in threats of hell-fire for those who did not pay their tithes. People were taught to believe that a scrupulous fulfillment of externals took care of all their religious duty. A soldier who abstained on Fridays and made regular offerings at the shrine of St. Barbara had no fears for the welfare of his soul if he died in battle, regardless of how many civilians he might rob or kill.[56] Erasmus perceived what is now commonplace among students of religion, that there is an inverse proportion between a magical and an ethical conception of religion. The fear of punishment made people scrupulous about ceremonies; the performance of these obligations made them secure in righteousness, so they could pursue their hatreds or indulge their passions in good conscience.

Erasmus believed that the words of the New Testament had power to heal the moral blindness of European society. Scripture was a great mystery, "a mere divine power." He who studied it with reverence would become a different man. In the words of the Gospels "Christ still lives, breathes and speaks, I almost said more efficaciously than when He walked among men."[57] Erasmus's praise of Scripture echoes sentiments that can be found in the writings of the Fathers. It seems also to be a variant of the humanist belief in the magic of language: as Christ was far greater than Cicero, so his words must be the most efficacious of all. More clearly humanist was Erasmus's contention that the original meaning of the New Testament had become obscured by a tangle of inept commentaries. Dialecticians hunting through St. Paul for quotations failed to notice that the author of the Epistle to the Romans could not have written the Epistle to the Hebrews. Theologians looking for support for the religion of ceremonies referred the words of John the Baptist—"Do Penance!"—to the sacrament of confession. Erasmus was able to show that the Greek word *metanoiete* meant an interior change of heart and not an external rite.[58] Thus critical scholarship could restore the original ethical or spiritual meaning of the text. Erasmus was greatly encouraged by a new emphasis on Greek and Hebrew at the universities. He also hoped that the Bible would be translated from the original into vernacular languages. At last the Word of God might be widely disseminated and clearly preached.[59]

He was confident that the Gospel would take effect because he believed that human nature would be instinctively receptive to it. Again and again he returned to the words of Christ in the eleventh chapter of Matthew: "Come to me all you who labor . . . for my yoke is easy and my burden light." The yoke to which Christ referred was the law of charity; it was easy to bear because it corresponded to man's deep longing for peace and friendship. Thus the law of nature was the law of Christ.[60] Just as Erasmus emphasized the gentle qualities of human nature, so he emphasized the mildness of Christ; in a moment of enthusiasm he even argued that Christ had never displayed anger. The Christ of Erasmus was meek and benevolent, like the Christ of contemporary Netherlands painters; perhaps he was more a product of Netherlands culture than he sometimes cared to admit.[61] But he was a humanist in his belief in man's readiness to respond to the gentle Christ. Once men could hear the true Gospel, free from ceremonies, they would desire of their own accord to follow Christ; they did not need threats or coercion. This was what St. Paul meant by Christian liberty. True followers of Christ would do more of their own will than they were required to do by the law. Once the Gospel could be purely preached and freely accepted, there would be less greed, less violence, and fewer wars.[62]

It can now be seen that Erasmus's critique of medieval religion has the same structure as his critique of contemporary education. In both cases coercion or constraint is an obstacle to virtue. Ceremonial obligations enforced by threats of eternal punishment, like lessons in logic enforced by threats of physical punishment, tended to produce bitter and violent men. In both cases Erasmus has great faith in the power of language—whether of Horace or of the Gospels—to bring about moral transformation. Finally, in both cases he believes that virtue can be achieved by encouraging instead of confining man's natural goodness—by an atmosphere of freedom instead of coercion. To make room for the natural eagerness of youth, schoolmasters must lay aside the book of rules; to make room for the promptings of natural piety, the church must change its laws so that ceremonies no longer bind under pain of sin.[63] It should be said again that there were other influences on Erasmus besides the humanist tradition. But his critique of medieval religion and education would not be intelligible without premises that derive from the humanist preoccupation with rhetoric and grammar. His achievement was to fuse ideas and attitudes of his humanist predecessors into a comprehensive and original critique of late medieval culture, based, it is true, on the somewhat narrow assumption that a culture is the end product of its formal and explicit systems of training. In 1517, just after the publication of his Greek New Testament, he could see a new generation of teachers and preachers on the horizon. Others trained in the new learning were taking responsible positions at princely courts. Erasmus dreamed that his program for the moral reformation of European society might become a reality; for a moment he saw the birth of a new Golden Age.[64] Perhaps no one has ever had greater faith in the power of education.

The dream of peaceful change was of course smashed to pieces in the tumult of the Protestant Reformation. Earlier in his career Erasmus had not been so hopeful as to demand that church laws be changed or relaxed. He asked only that educated Christians, who stood apart from the common herd, should have freedom to give a spiritual interpretation to ceremonial observances. But in the *Praise of Folly* (1511) he changed the significance of this conventional distinction between the common people and the intellectual elite: the philosophers, who cling to arid reason and despise ordinary emotions, are the real fools.[65] In the great scholarly works that follow, riding the crest of his fame, he declared that church laws must be changed or abolished so as to free laymen from the "tyranny" of the clergy.[66] The unspoken premise, however, was that the common people would still obey the authorities and would accept guidance from learned men. Hence the popular uprisings of the Reformation nudged Erasmus back toward the classical maxim that "the people is a great beast." In hopeful times he had written of the scholar's duty to proclaim the truth no matter what, especially in religion. But in 1522, two years before the terrible Peasants' War, he seemed willing to sacrifice part of the truth to preserve law and order. Even though the pope does not have all the powers that are claimed for him by some theologians, he suggested, it might be better if people were told that he did, for thus they would be more inclined to obey.[67] No moral teaching was more classical than the Platonic lie. As many have said,[68] the aristocratic character of Erasmus's humanist reform program helps to explain the fact that while the Reformation and the Counter-Reformation struck deep roots in popular culture, Erasmus was venerated only by a few intellectuals.

* * *

It is easy of course at a distance of four centuries to point out the naiveté of Erasmus's humanist optimism. One of the reasons why his name will survive this and probably subsequent commemorations is that he was indeed more than a humanist. He was able to discern some of the limitations of the humanist tradition even as he exploited its resources. This is clear, first, from the fact that he gradually overcame the conventional humanist prejudice against non-classical Latin. A disenchantment with the ideal of eloquence seems to have begun when certain Italian humanists in Venice suggested that he, a mere Dutchman, had not been able to master all the subtleties of a true classical style.[69] Back in England he apparently took more seriously John Colet's view that preaching should be free of rhetorical devices.[70] One of his prefaces to the New Testament praised the evangelists for writing simply, for it was not fitting for the Gospel to depend on human cleverness.[71] In later writings he asserted, contrary to his own former opinions, that the Latin of medieval scholastic writers could be just as good as anybody else's, that people would be stirred "more by an unstructured sermon which comes from an ardent soul than by a sermon fitted out with all the devices of the rhetoricians but which comes from the lips and not the heart." Even his own Latin style seems to have become simpler as he grew older.[72]

More significantly, he also advanced somewhat beyond the implications of his own naive optimism. His rosy vision of the future in 1517 was typically humanist insofar as humanists tended to believe in the moral improvement of mankind through a calm and peaceful process of education. He was puzzled and hurt by hostile reactions to his New Testament that arose later that same year. He could only surmise that there must be a conscious plot on the part of the friars to destroy his reforming ideas in order to preserve their own tyranny. Johann Pfefferkorn, a converted Jew who was attacking the German humanist Johann Reuchlin for his Hebrew studies, was in reality still a Jew: he was deliberately stirring up internal dissension among Christians in order to win favor with his own people. Jerome Aleander, the papal legate who suspected a connection between Erasmus and Luther, was likewise a Jew in disguise. Erasmus's letters in 1519 and 1520 are filled with references to the great monkish-Jewish conspiracy.[73] This reaction is a measure or index of his original naiveté. Like most northern humanists he had no experience of practical affairs. He had no sense of the intractableness of things, nor of the stormy, nonintellectual character of many of the forces which bring change. He was utterly unprepared for the violent outcry that greeted his own works, much less for the greater storm that soon gathered around Luther. Consequently he was driven to an explanation that fitted his own narrow understanding: the trouble must have been caused by evil men conspiring against him.

The magnitude of events soon forced him to realize that no mere personal explanations would suffice. In 1521, after his effort to prevent a rupture between Luther and Rome had proven futile, he began to speak less of conspiracy and more of tragedy. He had found in Homer and Euripides a literary clue that gave him some perspective. The *ate* or rage unleashed by the quarrel between Agamemnon and Achilles in the *Iliad* was a force stronger than reason. Similarly, the selfish rage of the friars had provoked Luther to respond with equal fury; preachers on both sides made inflammatory appeals and popular anger and resentment snapped the fragile bonds of restraint.[74] In such circumstances no human power, much less the gentle persuasion of reason, could bring events under control. This tragedy was a punishment for the sins of Christians; it would end peacefully only if God himself somehow intervened, as in the *deus-ex-machina* endings of Euripides.[75] In light of this view of things Erasmus became less confident about assigning blame. He still felt that the real trouble had been started by clergymen who were protecting their own vested interests. But he now saw that indulgences and other practices which he had attacked had been introduced originally for a reasonable purpose and not as instruments of clerical tyranny. Their evil consequences had simply not been foreseen.[76] Thus human reason was mocked not only by tragic outbreaks of passion but also by the movement of time itself.

Erasmus was still not a fatalist. If ever passions could be calmed, he believed the doctrinal differences between Catholics and Lutherans could be resolved by discussions between carefully chosen men of learning. Those who might think he was hopelessly naive on this point as well should remember that Catholic and Lutheran spokesmen did agree on the doctrine of justification at the Regensburg Colloquy of 1541.[77] But as time went on passions only intensified. Recognizing that his modulated tones would not be heard among the din of voices Erasmus fell silent. From his own day to the present many have accused him of cowardice for not committing himself to one side or the other. His dear friend Thomas More overlooked abuses in the Catholic Church in order to attack the Reformers with all possible vigor. Other friends, like John Oecolampadius in Basel, became pillars of the Protestant cause. But the humanism of Erasmus meant not merely that man is the measure of all things but that measure is the mark of man's humanity. Neither the doctrines of Luther nor the authority of the pope could justify religious hatred among the followers of Christ. Once the Reformation and the Counter-Reformation had become a part of history it was easy to look back on his growing isolation as the tragedy of Erasmus.[78] But to Erasmus, who had the courage to remain alone in his convictions, the course of events could only be understood as the tragedy of Christendom.

Erasmus as Reformer

By Lewis W. Spitz

A well-known historian, Lewis W. Spitz has been conspicuous in altering and deepening our appreciation of the Northern Renaissance. He entered into his impressive literary and academic career upon graduating from Concordia College and Seminary, the University of Missouri, and Harvard University. After an initial appointment at the University of Missouri, Professor Spitz became an associate, later full, professor of history at Stanford University. Since 1967, he has also been the American managing editor of the *Archive for Reformation History*. Among his many distinguished publications, the most important are: *Conrad Celtis: The German Arch-humanist* (Cambridge: Harvard University Press, 1957); *Religious Renaissance of the German Humanists* (Cambridge: Harvard University Press, 1963); *Life in Two Worlds: Biography of William Sihler* (St. Louis: Concordia, 1968); *The Protestant Reformation* (Englewood Cliffs, New Jersey: Prentice-Hall, 1966); *The Reformation: Material or Spiritual* (Boston: D. C. Heath, 1962). Moreover, a long list of provocative articles have appeared regularly in such journals as *Church History, Journal of the History of Ideas, Archive for Reformation History,* and *Studies in the Renaissance*. In recognition of these extraordinary achievements, Dr. Spitz has been awarded fellowships by the Guggenheim Memorial Foundation, the American Council of Learned Societies, the National Endowment for the Humanities, and the Henry E. Huntington Library as well as a Fulbright Lectureship at the University of Mainz.

In the year 1557 a certain Bartholomäus Kalkreuter of Krossen delivered an academic address in Wittenberg University which included a panegyric on Erasmus. Erasmus does not need to be lauded any more than Hercules or Cyrus, he declared. The youth should be encouraged to read his useful writings and to consider his many virtues and the talent given him by God. He praised his keen sense of discovery, his insight and perspective in the choice of material and of sentences, the wealth of his oral expression, his brilliant pictures, the beauty and spirit of his presentation, in which he so distinguished himself that it could appear as though the graces themselves had from all sides strewn his speech with flowers. His life, too, contained many examples of his virtues, his diligence, patience in need, modesty, and beneficence. His edition of the New Testament was a work to which he was led by divine grace. He contributed greatly to the reawakening of the Greek and Latin languages. "Since therefore," the young speaker concluded, "Erasmus possessed a great power of genius and many outstanding virtues, and since he in the highest degree promoted the language study necessary to the church and the state, we wish to preserve his memory in a thankful heart, to read his literary monuments, and to acknowledge him gratefully."[1] The special charm of this address is that it had been prepared for young Bartholomäus by a sixty-year-old professor, the great reformer Philipp Melanchthon. Twenty-one years after the death of the prince of the humanists Luther's closest associate and successor as titular head of the Reformation movement paid this tribute to Erasmus, in whom he recognized a kindred reformatory spirit.

I *Erasmus the Reformer*

The ambiguity of Erasmus's relation to the Reformation has tended to obscure the fact that Erasmus was a reformer in his own right and in his own way. The very ambivalence of his position was rooted both in his complex psychology and in his insistence upon maintaining his own program above and independent of all parties. A rough-hewn man such as Frederick the Wise of Saxony experienced real difficulty in sizing up Erasmus, a curious little man, he thought, for one never quite knows how one stands with him.

Erasmus lacked robustness and preferred to avoid conflict by dissembling, when confronted by opponents. He was a valetudinarian, concerned for his physical welfare, and an intellectual, fretting over his good name and scholarly reputation. When his pride was injured or his professional reputation in jeopardy, he could counterattack with deft, rapier-like thrusts. He could also move in close and scratch in an almost feminine, or at any rate feline, fashion. But he preferred to present himself in such a way as to avoid conflict, until put upon by an Edward Lee, Jacob Zuñiga (Stunica), Johann Eck, or Martin Dorp. Moreover, Erasmus was extremely sensitive to his environment and open to immediate impressions. He genuinely saw so much positive good in the ideas of other men as he encountered them that he developed an empathy with various parties. Thus with the humanists his "manner and his conversation were polished, affable, and even charming," as the young Erasmian Beatus Rhenanus noted. With Catholic dignitaries he gave every appearance of being a good churchman. With the reformers he could converse with feeling about the *philosophia evangelica*. The German philosopher Schopenhauer once asked whether it is necessary to deceive the living in order to praise the dead. Even an intellectual giant and outsized man of history such as Erasmus had his weaknesses which cannot be concealed.[2] On the positive side, as the "man in the middle" seeking to reconcile and pacify diametrically opposed parties, Erasmus could hardly avoid giving the appearance of a man with a foot in each camp. This awkward stance was difficult to maintain and easily subject to misinterpretation. "I have become," he once complained, "a heretic to both sides."

Small wonder that his biographers and the historians have seen him in such very contradictory ways. Three essentially different analyses of Erasmus dominate the historiographical landscape. The first of these depicts him as a person of weak character, whose timidity and lack of character prevented him from accepting the consequences of his own premises. This was the Erasmus who confessed that he did not have the strength for martyrdom. Christianity, he opined, has had many martyrs but few scholars. He feared that if put to the test, he, like Peter, would deny Christ. Erasmus was conscious of his weaknesses and more ready to concede his faults than are many men. It is quite a simple matter to put together a mosaic of such expressions that portrays him as a little man concerned about his reputation, a trimmer who was a Protestant at heart, but who conformed to Catholicism in order to retain ecclesiastical support and other perquisites.

The second common way of viewing Erasmus is as a devotee of reason, a modernist who was a forerunner of the Enlightenment.[3] Scholars of this opinion see Erasmian humanism as a progressive philosophy which was temporarily submerged by the

Protestant and Catholic intensely theological reformations, but
which emerged again in the Englightenment to help shape the modern world.

A third view of Erasmus, current during his own lifetime, waş
that he was a forerunner of Luther's Reformation. Luther himself
spoke of the revival of learning as a John the Baptist preparing the
way for the coming of the gospel. Erasmus was a harsh critic of
the church, he promoted humanist learning against scholastic
theology, he advanced the study of the Biblical languages and
criticized the Vulgate, and with his Christocentrism he subverted
the sacramental-sacerdotal system. Luther, in the eyes of many
orthodox opponents of Erasmus, merely took the second step of
adopting Pauline Christology. This in itself established his guilt
by association, as they saw it. A charade performed in the presence
of Emperor Charles V showed a man enter the stage and unload
from his back a bundle of sticks, Johannes Reuchlin. A second
man followed and arranged the sticks into an inflammable pile,
Erasmus. A third man entered and set the wood on fire, Luther.
"Erasmus laid the egg that Luther hatched" was a saying popular
during his own lifetime.

There is a certain truth in each of these ways of looking at
Erasmus, for seldom do we see any man, living or dead, whole,
as he is in all dimensions of his being. But Erasmus can be seen
in yet another way, as a reformer with his own serious program
for the renewal of the church and the improvement of society.
Understood in this light Erasmus appears as a man with an inte-
grated personality and a great unity of purpose directing his life.
The tools with which he undertook to build a new platform of reform were the tools of scholarship, philology, and historico-critical
study. The material with which he worked were the ancient sources
of Christian antiquity, the Scriptures, and the Greek and Latin
patristic writings. From these sources he derived his *philosophia
Christi,* a non-dogmatic, Christocentric form of spirituality which
he hoped could be taught to the learned and brought to the simple
in such a way as to infuse new life into all Christendom. Erasmus
held to this program from the early optimistic days when he
could write to Wolfgang Capito (1517), "I anticipate the near
approach of a golden age," to the bitter end, when he dragged his
sick body back to a death-bed in Basel. His constancy of purpose

against all adversity and despite the most scurrilous attacks from all sides marks him as a man of courage, and perseverance. He envisioned a reformed Christendom in which men would follow the Master in faith and love, in which the church would be restored to the simplicity and purity of its early days, and in which the nations of the earth would live together in peace and brotherhood.[4]

II *Erasmus the Critic*

It is ironic that Petrarch, the father of humanism, should be most widely known for his sonnets, Machiavelli for his little *Prince,* and Erasmus for his *Praise of Folly.* He wrote this *encomium Moriae* as a casual piece while a houseguest of Sir Thomas More upon his return from Italy. It has through the centuries appeared in more than six hundred editions. In it he punctured human foibles and pretence in all walks of life. Some of his sharpest thrusts were directed against abuses within the church and against monks, scholastic doctors, and high churchmen. "We have praised Folly," he observed in the preface, "not quite foolishly."

In the *Colloquies,* which have seen three hundred editions, he provided a panorama of popular church life which was anything but edifying. He began the *Colloquies* quite innocently like the *De duplica copia* as a practice aid to Latin style and fluency, but they gradually grew into a comprehensive commentary on the culture of the times. They gave lively expression to his critical ideas and, because of the constant additions and revisions, they provide an informative pictograph of his changing moods through the years. In the edition of 1526 criticism of abuses within the church reached a crescendo with the addition of four colloquies attacking racketeering and superstitions. Even though Erasmus and Luther had exchanged their diatribes on the question of free will, Erasmus still mentioned Luther and Zwingli with approval. He heaped scorn upon the louse-bitten obscurantist monks and poured out contempt upon the pedantic scholastic doctors who spoiled theology with their over-refined distinctions. The scholastics were quibblers and "word players," syllogism manipulators, logic choppers, and pedantic abusers of the Latin language. Samuel Butler's lines on a pedantic logician in *Hudibras* might well have been penned by Erasmus:

> He was in Logic, a great critic,
> Profoundly skilled in analytic;
> He could distinguish, and divide,
> A hair 'twixt south and southwest side.

With his background in the nonspeculative religion of the *devotio moderna* and under the influence of Vitrier and Colet, he had little patience with the dialectical method in theology. But like Lorenzo Valla, his intellectual forebear, he always maintained a charitable appreciation of Thomas Aquinas. Beyond criticism, Erasmus commented, he intended his *Colloquies* to contain "That which would conduce to the formation of character." His positive program could be discerned even in those writings most critical in tone. The great Dutch cultural historian Johann Huizinga once commented that Erasmus was his most brilliant and profound when he was being humorous in an ironic way.

III   *Erasmus the Scholar*

The young humanist Urbanus Rhegius praised Erasmus as the "first author of the renaissance of theology." Erasmus never considered himself to be a theologian in the technical sense of a professional qualified to teach in a theological faculty. But as a Biblical scholar and student of historical theology, he was as much a theologian as the scholastic doctors with their dialectical innovations. Innovations, for Erasmus looked to older sources for his theology, to the Scriptures and the writings of the *prisci theologi,* the devout and learned patristic writers. "I had rather be a pious theologian with Chrysostom than an invincible one with Scotus," he declared.

In 1516, as a forty-seven-year-old scholar at the height of his powers, Erasmus scored his greatest publishing triumph, his edition of the New Testament in Greek. The Greek edition became the text from which Luther preached his sermons. Between the years 1517 and 1524, he did a paraphrase on the entire New Testament, except the book of Revelation, which mystified him. The *Paraphrases* in a 1548 translation were placed in every parish church in England where they contributed their part to the moderate Anglican reform.

The great philosopher Leibniz once replied, when he had been asked to edit a text, "Do you not know that asking me to become an editor is like marrying your best friend to a shrew?" Erasmus, a celibate cleric, was married to just such a shrew. For he devoted his life to Herculean editorial efforts, bringing to the world of learning classical texts and patristic writings. He called his study in Basel a "mill" where, "standing on one foot" at his writing stand, he ground out scholarly editions, learned prefaces, translations, and commentaries for eight years in the period of his greatest productivity.

Erasmus in the tradition of the Italian humanists did editions of classical Latin and Greek authors, Cicero, Seneca, Quintus Curtius, Suetonius, Pliny, the Elder, Livy, Terence and Lucian. Lucian, as Erasmus wrote to Archbishop William of Canterbury, is always good for a laugh. Erasmus did translations of Galen, Xenophon, and Plutarch and Greek editions of Demosthenes and Aristotle.

But Erasmus made his greatest contribution to the world of learning and religion with his editions of the church fathers. Jerome, patron saint of the Brethren of the Common Life, was Erasmus's model of a learned churchman. He lavished much care and affection upon his nine-volume edition of Jerome (1516), as though to make things up to the saint for his textual emendations of the Vulgate. The edition was an immediate and great success. He pressed on with the Latin Cyprian in 1520, the Pseudo-Arnobius in 1522, Hilary in 1523, Ambrose in 1527, and Augustine in 1528.

Even more important for the Western world was Erasmus's publication of editions and translations of the Greek fathers. Italian humanists such as Ambrogio Traversari had made a modest beginning. Lorenzo Valla and the humanists of his century had appealed to Christian antiquity as an arsenal to use against scholasticism and by way of support for their own modes of thought and cultural pursuits.[5] But Erasmus as a Northern Christian humanist moved in on Greek patristic literature like a conquering hero. He published Irenaeus in Latin in 1526. He did Chrysostom in Latin in 1530. He edited Basil in Greek in 1532, the first Greek author ever printed in the Empire. He did a number of translations from Athanasius. In 1536 he labored on an edition of Origen in Latin nearly until the time of his death. In his *Life of St. Jerome* Erasmus had discussed his plan to restore these ancient treasures

to the church. By the end of his life he had made tremendous
strides toward achieving his goal.[6]

IV   *Erasmus the Constructive Theologian*

Erasmus intended his critical cuts at the evils in society and
church to clear away the thickets and to prepare the way for this
philosophia Christi which would inspire renewal and reform. True
theology required a return to the pure gospel. Simplicity should
replace complexity and inward spirituality should supplant external
rote performance of religious duties. Christ's teachings and His
example should become the guide and inspiration for life.

Erasmus was no systematician and it is necessary to read widely
in his prefaces, treatises, and letters to appreciate the full range
of his moralistic spiritualism. But the most characteristic expression of his religious thought is to be found in three treatises, the
Enchiridion militis Christiani, the Paraclesis, and the *Ratio seu
Methodus.* The *Enchiridion,* a "dagger handbook" of the Christian
knight, written in 1501 and published two years later, was written
at the request of a good lady who was concerned about the soul
of her husband John, an ill-tempered roughneck soldier. The
Enchiridion emphasized the need for good morals based upon
genuine Christian love. It described as worthless the performance
of merely outward forms of religion and such practices as fasting,
the invocation of saints, indulgences, or pilgrimages. It was highly
moralistic and drained Christianity of its apocalyptic and deeply
mystical elements.

In the *Paraclesis* or *Exhortation,* the Introduction to his New
Testament, he expressed regret that Christians were less articulate
about the teachings of their faith than the adherents of many
philosophies such as Platonism, Pythagoreanism, Stoicism, Cyni-
cism, or Epicureanism. He disagreed strongly with those who do
not want the divine Scriptures to be read by the uneducated, as
though the defense of the Christian religion were based upon
ignorance of it. He wrote:

It may be better to conceal the mysteries of kings, but Christ
would have His mysteries published as widely as possible. I wish that
all, even the lowliest of women, would read the Gospel, would read
Paul's epistles. O that these were translated into all languages of all

[people], so that they could be read and understood not only by the Scotsmen and the Irish, but also by the Turks and the Saracens! The first step surely is to get to know it in some way. Though many may deride, some may be won. O that the farmer would sing something of this at the plow, the weaver would hum something of this at the shuttle, the traveler would lighten the tedium of his journey with tales of this kind! Let all discourses of all Christians be of these things!

The simple evangelical counsels are the heart of the gospel and if a ditch-digger teaches and practices them, he is a great theologian. The New Testament presents to the reader the living image of Christ's most sacred mind and Christ himself, speaking, healing, dying, rising, and render Him totally present in such a way that one would see Him less if one were to see Him before one's eyes. In the *Ratio seu Methodus* or "Method of Theology" Erasmus expanded the inspired sentences of the *Paraclesis* into a fuller statement of his Christocentric moral philosophy.

Erasmus was orthodox on trinitarian dogma and held formally to a high Christology. His attitudes toward the church's teachings on the sacraments were consistently correct, and his expressions conservative especially during his last years. But he gave a strong moralistic emphasis to the meaning of Christ's life and teaching. With this moralistic strain and the nonspeculative cast of his thought he combined a Platonic spiritualistic interpretation of St. Paul. The key to his thought is the Pauline passage "the letter kills, but the Spirit makes alive." In exegesis he preferred a spiritual interpretation of the text to a literal or historico-critical interpretation. In morals it is the heart, not the outward act that makes a thing good or bad. In religion it is the inward spirit and not the external rite that matters. This highly spiritualistic approach to theology received powerful reinforcement from his reading of Greek Fathers such as Gregory Nazianzen and Clement of Alexandria. He also derived from the Fathers a universalistic outlook which enabled him to hope fervently for the salvation of wise and noble pagans.

V   *Humanist Reformer and the Reformation*

The role of Erasmus as reformer was not over in 1517, 1525, or in 1536. The Reformation proved to be a mightier movement than the Renaissance with more radical ecclesiastical and sociological consequences. History passed Erasmus by with Luther's emergence onto the scene. Erasmus's and Luther's dramatic controversy over the question of free will has often been taken as the final word on Erasmus and the Reformation. It is often depicted as the watershed between the humanist and the evangelical reformations. The truth is more complex and interesting, for Erasmus lived on as a reformer through his influence upon the mainline magisterial Reformation as well as upon individual free spirits. What is true of Erasmus as a single person, though an outsize man of history, is true of the whole humanist movement. The relation of the Renaissance, as the "most intractable problem child of historiography," to the Middle Ages is far better understood than its relation to the historical period which followed, the Reformation. Only a revisionist interpretation of the big problem of historical relation and interaction will enable us to assess intelligently Erasmus's role as a reformer even after his break with Luther and his death twelve years later.

Scholars are familiar with the classic exchange of Wilhelm Dilthey and Ernst Troeltsch about the place of the Renaissance and Reformation in the total sweep of Western history.[7] Dilthey viewed the Renaissance and Reformation as complementary sources of modernity, the Reformation was the religious expression of the Renaissance. Troeltsch thought the Reformation, as a revival of medieval religiosity, was in fact antithetical to the artistically ennobled naturalism of the Renaissance. The Reformation with its roots in deep veins of popular belief proved to be stronger than the aristocratic and elitist Renaissance, which went underground to emerge once again in the Enlightenment. The power of the church and of Protestantism was not, Troeltsch conceded, a purely contrary and destructive one, for by means of the weakening, refraction, and assimilating transformation the Renaissance "became a world culture and permeated all the pores of high society." Scholarship has long since substantially revised the Burckhardtian retrospective vision of the Renaissance, bringing out the genuine religious concerns of the Italian humanists, yes, also those of Erasmus's model, Lorenzo Valla. Scholarship needs now to take note of the fact that the magisterial reformers and their successors assumed a positive stance toward the cultural treasures of the Renaissance. The humanist disciplines were not reluctantly accommodated and grudgingly or craftily assimilated, but gladly embraced, enthusiastically sanctioned, and energetically promoted in publications and through education. The ongoing influence of Erasmus is everywhere in evidence and is easily detected. The good men do lives after them!

To document the affirmative response of both mainline Protestantism and a major sector of the reformed Catholic intellectual world to the cultural content of Renaissance humanism would require not only an article triple the length of this one, but a book to begin with and a library to complete the task.[8] Here a few suggestions must suffice with a somewhat mechanical division of the subject matter, as a method, Bodin would say, for "the easy comprehension of history."

The Renaissance humanists set in opposition to the much maligned scholastic learning a body of ancient classical and Christian literature, a set of disciplines, and, contained in both, a system of values characteristically their own. They embraced the liberal arts and the classical languages, they developed an approach to education designed to transmit these arts effectively and to develop the young as complete persons. They promoted grammar, rhetoric, and poetry in conscious opposition to the old dialectic. While there were definite limitations in the writing and professional cultivation of history, they contributed mightily to the development of a historical sense.[9] They revised and in important ways reversed the medieval approach to law. They went back to the sources of Christian antiquity in the Scriptures and the patristic writings. They stressed moral philosophy, very often an ethical Paulinism tinged with Platonism. A feeling of responsibility toward the state, whether civic humanism in a republican sense, or princely government in a traditional sense, was a constant in their social philosophy. They were Christocentric in theology, though seldom expressly Christological in a Pauline sense in their soteriology. These phrases characterize, I hold, the mainstream of that complex, protean, and multifaceted phenomenon called Renaissance humanism.[10]

During the Reformation period these major intellectual and cultural emphases were not only passively assimilated and transmitted, but were enthusiastically embraced and then advanced. Admittedly there were anti-intellectual groups and cultural atavists hostile to the new learning, but the overriding response was positive. Young Philipp Melanchthon made the keynote address in his inaugural lecture at Wittenberg "On Improving the Studies of the Youth" (1518). He demeaned medieval culture, berated the sophists, and called for a revival of the "letters of reborn culture *(studium renascentium litterarum)*."[11] He urged the whole humanist curriculum, rhetoric, Greek and Hebrew letters, history, philosophy, and science, and pledged to devote himself to teaching with all his energies. For all his interest in theology, he remained a professor in the arts faculty to the end of his career.[12]

This inaugural address is only one of the many powerful orations praising the liberal arts and validating humanist learning for the Reformation world. A stress on classical languages and the cultural good which they convey is always a major emphasis. Peter Mosellanus, the little man whom Luther had favored over Melanchthon for the Wittenberg position, delivered such an address at Leipzig University, *An Oration Concerning the Knowledge of Various Languages Which Must Be Esteemed.*[13] Mosellanus's great moment came when he delivered the oration on *The Right Method of Disputing* before the Leipzig Debate in 1519. Melanchthon and Joachim Camerarius were present when the frail but spirited Mosellanus died at an early age and grieved deeply over his loss. Camerarius developed himself into one of the most prolific humanist scholars in Protestant Leipzig. Two of his public addresses typical of his humanist enthusiasm combined with evangelical fervor were his *Oration on the Study of Good Letters and the Arts and of the Greek and Latin Languages* and an *Oration Concerning the Cultivation of Piety and of Virtue by the Studies of Good Arts.*[14] Camerarius as a lifelong friend of Melanchthon wrote the best contemporary biography of him.

To shift the focus for a moment to Geneva, just as Luther took the initiative in establishing the humanist curriculum at Wittenberg, so Calvin promoted the founding of the Academy, later The University of Geneva. The twenty-seven weekly lectures offered included three in theology, eight in Hebrew, three in Greek in ethics and five in Greek orators or poets, three in physics or mathematics, five in dialectic or rhetoric. Calvin's comrade and later successor Theodore Beza, a professor of Greek himself, delivered the *Address at the Solemn Opening of the Academy in Geneva,* praising the good arts and the disciplines. It is well known that Calvin's own Latin teacher, Mathurin Cordier (1480–1564), the author of Erasmian-like colloquies and Latin instruction books, ended his days in Geneva.

At no time in history, except perhaps our own, has so much been written about educational theory and practice as in the Renaissance. The volume increased rather than diminished during the Reformation era, and the message was even more intense. The Reformers went beyond the humanists, urging that every child be made literate through universal compulsory education. The content of academy learning was to be classical. The vocation of the teacher was held to be as divine as that of the preacher. Luther's powerful writings on education are well known. Ulrich Zwingli's *Of the Upbringing and Education of Youth in Good Manners and Christian Discipline*[15] was in this humanist tradition. "Rank, beauty and wealth are not genuine riches, for they are subject to chance," he concludes. "The only true adornments are virtue and honor." Melanchthon's role in promoting secondary schools with a classical curriculum was crucial. In his *Oration in Praise of a New School, Delivered at Nuremberg in an Assembly of Very Learned Men and Nearly the Entire Senate* (1526) he exclaimed: "For what else brings greater benefits to the whole human race than letters? No art, no work, not, by Hercules, the very fruits born of the earth, not, finally, this sun, which many have believed is the author of life, is as necessary as the knowledge of letters."[16] The greatest of all Protestant educators, Johannes Sturm, not only directed the famous school at Strassburg, but wrote a small library of books on education, all advancing the humanist program for a nobility of letters.[17] The great English educator Roger Ascham, tutor of Queen Elizabeth I, was a devoted admirer of Sturm and even named an unlucky son in his honor.

The Reformers emulated the humanists in promoting grammar, rhetoric, and poetry. Melanchthon's grammar was typical of many. "Much ruin happened to the church," he observed, "through the decline of grammar."[18] His *Encomium on Eloquence* or *Declamation on the Absolute Necessity of the Art of Speaking to Every Kind of Studies* expressed his unconditional acceptance of humanist rhetorical theory.[19] He saw man, as did the humanists, as a living creature unique for his power of speech. Whether it was Camerarius's notes on the orations of Cicero or Sturm's two books on the lost art of speaking, the epigoni carried on this rhetorical tradition.[20] From Eobanus Hessus to Johannes Secundus Everardus, Micyllus, and Calvinist poets of France, poetic culture persisted.[21]

Leonardo Bruni and other humanists had assigned first place to history for its pragmatic value in moral instruction. Whatever their failings in the writing and professional teaching of history on the university level, they still theoretically held it to be of great value, philosophy teaching by example. The reformers adopted the humanist pragmatic interpretation and application of history. Luther, attracted increasingly, under Melanchthon's influence, to humanist subjects, wrote prefaces to the historical works and editions of Galeatius Capella, Lazarus Spengler, Georg Spalatin, Robert Barnes, and others. Melanchthon wrote his *Chronicon* and his famous prefaces to Caspar Hedio and Johann Cuspinian's histories. Camerarius did a Latin edition of Thucydides and his own histories. And a Lutheran trained in the classics fastened the term *medium aevum* upon historiography. The humanist historical approach to law supported by a lofty conception of the dignity and divine sanction of law received a hearty endorsement from the reformers.[22]

In the drive to the sources in the Scriptures and Christian antiquity the Reformers followed down the trail blazed by the Christian humanists. The Leipzig debate, the Sacramentarian controversy and other events precipitated the serious study of the church fathers as witnesses to the *primum et verum,* the teaching on justification offered by the Scriptures as *Norma Normans.* The modest beginnings in patristic studies by the Italian humanists and the great advances made by Northern humanists were carried to new heights by scholars both Protestant and Catholic in the centuries which followed. Luther offered a preface to accompany Georg Major's *Lives of the Fathers.*[23] Melanchthon offered advice in his "little patrology" on "the discernment with which Augustine, Ambrose, Origen, and other teachers ought to be read."[24] The confessions were laced with the testimonies of the fathers.[25]

In theology itself, the special emphases of Christian humanism in terms of its Christocentricity, spiritualism, and anthropology made an impact upon major reformers such as Zwingli and Melanchthon.[26] The precepts and maxims offered to the youth by way of instruction in moral philosophy correspond closely to the familiar aphorisms of the earlier period.[27] More important still, the humanist component in the so-called "mediating theology" (*Vermittlungstheologie*) of Georg Major and in the latitudinarian wing of the Reformed Churches became a moving force in ecclesiastical history.

There was no *Erasmus redivivus* in the eighteenth century, for Erasmus never died anymore than did Shakespeare before his mythical "rediscovery."[28] His influence as a humanist reformer lived on in the mainstream of Reformation thought. His *Folly* and *Colloquies* were not the only works of his to see many new editions during the sixteenth and seventeenth centuries. His *Adages* and *Apothegmes,* his *Querela Pacis* and the *De contemptu mundi,* his *De duplici copia verborum ac rerum* and his treatise on the *Pater Noster,* his *Enchiridion* and his *Paraphrases,* his *Exposition of the Creed* and treatise on *The Preparation for Death,* his *Paraclesis,* all were republished, read, and cited. Often they were published in omnibus volumes together with works of the reformers. Erasmus in death lived up to his motto "Concedo nulli," I yield to none.[29]

Melanchthon was a major link in this concatenation of intellectual influence.[30] That, then, is the significance of the panegyric of Erasmus delivered so long after his death by the obscure academician, Bartholomäus Kalkreuter of Krossen. Nor would Erasmus, who knew the power of the written as well as of the spoken word, have been surprised at the ongoing effect of his reformatory work. In his *Life of St. Jerome* Erasmus had described his plan to restore the ancient treasures of the Church and affirmed his faith in the inherent dynamism and thrust of truth itself. "Although the artisan can bring out the sparkle and luster of any jewel," he declared, "no imitation ever comes to possess the inner quality of a jewel. Truth has its own energy which no artifice can equal." [31]

Erasmus and His Place in History

By JOHN C. OLIN

A member of the Fordham University faculty since 1946, John C. Olin is presently Professor of Modern European History. In recent years, Professor Olin has established himself as a leading authority on the Catholic Reformation. After graduating from Canisius College and Fordham University, he completed his doctorate at Columbia University. As editor, Dr. Olin has published the following major works: *Christian Humanism and the Reformation: Selected Writings of Erasmus* (New York: Harper Torchbooks, 1965); *Calvin & Sadoleto: A Reformation Debate* (New York: Harper Torchbooks, 1966); *The Catholic Reformation: Savonarola to Ignatius Loyola* (New York: Harper & Row, 1969); *Luther, Erasmus and the Reformation: A Catholic-Protestant Reappraisal* (New York: Fordham University Press, 1969).

In approaching the topic I have been asked to speak about today—Erasmus and his place in history—an initial question immediately arose. What exactly is "a place in history?" Without allowing myself to become engrossed in speculation concerning the nature and meaning of history I resolved the query by concluding that for all practical purposes "a place in history" means simply the judgment or evaluation rendered by posterity on an important person and on his life and work. The question thus reduced itself in my mind to the subject of what others have thought about Erasmus. Now since it is largely the business of historians to think—extensively at least and professionally—about the past, my topic seemed to center on what historians have written about Erasmus, on how they have interpreted and appraised his role in the course of events. And this I have taken for my theme. We might call it "Erasmus and the historians." Or perhaps it would be more accurate to say "Erasmus in the view of some modern historians," since I do intend to limit my subject and select the examples I shall offer from a very considerable body of historical writing. Such, of course, is inevitable. The recent or current literature on Erasmus alone is a very formidable mass. It affords some confirmation perhaps of Colet's famous dictum that the name of Erasmus will never die.

Is this a valid way of tackling the problem of Erasmus's place in history? I think it is, and I offer two very brief arguments in my behalf. One concerns the nature of history itself. History is after of our *knowledge* of the past. A man's place in history then is our understanding or appreciation of his role. There must be, of course, some objectivity, some reasonable grounds, some careful analysis of the available evidence, but the subjective element is very strong, and the historian will approach the past with his own limitations, his own frame of reference, his own sense of relevancy and value. He will tell us in the final analysis only what he *thinks* the contribution or importance of a historical figure is. There may be broad consensus and apparently very firm grounds for the appraisal, but it remains a human judgment subject to correction and revision. In saying this I underline, as you will note, the fact that history is not a static phenomenon or an interpretation fixed for all time. Our subject then tends inevitably to become historiographical, that is, a matter of examining the views and evaluations of various historians.

My second argument is of a different character and not quite so cogent. It is from authority. Preserved Smith, the late distinguished professor of history at Cornell and a renowned scholar of the Reformation of a generation or more ago, wrote a very substantial biography of Erasmus. The final chapter in this work he entitled "The Genius of Erasmus and His Place in History," and he devoted the chapter to the views and opinions of a number of historians and other scholars on Erasmus. I shall follow his lead in this instance and present a comparable but more recent version of history's judgment.

*   *   *

In the case of history's great figures one often finds a variety of judgment and interpretation, and frequently there is sharp division of opinion, even contradictory views, regarding an individual's role or influence. That situation is fairly commonplace. But in Erasmus's case the interpretative variation as well as the controversy is especially marked. It was so in his own day, and it has continued at least to some extent down to ours. There are reasons, of course, that account for this, aside from the limited and subjective character of historical judgment. At the outset I should like to speak briefly about these factors.

For one thing, Erasmus, as you are well aware, lived and worked in a period of serious religious crisis and schism, the most serious perhaps that ever divided Western Christendom. We need hardly elaborate on the intensity of this division. As Europe's leading scholar and intellectual light he was involved in these events by virtue of the character of his work, the thrust of his purpose, and his influence. Yet from the start he resisted alignment or identification with any party or faction in the controversy. He had his point of view and his convictions, but he sought to rise above dogmatic argument lest it contribute to division and deepen the breach within the Church. His efforts were directed toward moderating the quarrel and ending the schism that developed. As a result he fell afoul of both extremes. In his *Compendium vitae* of early 1524 he tells us that "the Lutheran tragedy had burdened him with unbearable ill will" and that "he was torn apart by each faction, while he sought to serve the best interests of each." [1] That same year he wrote to his good friend John Fisher, the Bishop of Rochester: "Indeed, I war on three fronts: against these pagan Romans, who are meanly jealous of me; against certain theologians and friars, who use every stone at hand to bring me down; against some rabid Lutherans, who snarl at me because— so they say—I alone delay their own triumphs." [2] Erasmus had his critics before the "Luthern tragedy," but it was the enormously divisive and polarizing consequences of the controversy that now developed that caught him in the middle and "tore him apart."

We shall not retell here the story of Erasmus's attitude or role in the midst of the religious crisis.[3] Our intention is simply to call attention to the situation that involved him and to the effect it had on the way men viewed and judged him. Luther, for example, came to despise him. From his early attitude that Erasmus did not "promote the cause of Christ and God's grace sufficiently," Luther progressed to his scathing attack on him as a skeptic who "oozed

Lucian from every pore" in his *De servo arbitrio* of 1525.[4] And the Wittenberg prophet in his later years continued to denounce Erasmus as a scoffer, a pagan, and an enemy of the Gospel.[5] The other side was also relentless in its attack on him. He was seen to be in collusion with Luther and to have laid the egg Luther hatched. Jerome Aleander, papal legate to the court of Charles V in 1520–21 and a noted humanist scholar and former friend of Erasmus, denounced him to Rome as the real instigator of the heresy and disorder that now troubled Europe.[6] His writings were judged to be dangerous and subversive and full of error. A climax was reached in this onslaught against him by his Catholic opponents in 1558 when the fierce and frantic Paul IV (once a friend who had encouraged his scholarly endeavors) declared him a heretic *primae classis* and placed all his works on the papal Index.[7]

The unhappy situation that engulfed Erasmus was due not only to the schism, but also to the character of his thought and the nature of what he had to say. His goal was reform; he did seek to renew theology and the Christian life through a scriptural revival; he did attack those who blocked the way—the theologians of the schools and the mendicant friars whose Christian profession he felt was an empty and shameless thing. But the reform he sought challenged neither basic dogma nor essential institution and could not be equated with the preaching and the thrust of Luther and the Protestants against the entire fabric of the existing Church. Erasmus does not leave us in any doubt about this. Commenting on Luther's teaching in 1524 Erasmus wrote: "This contains many points which I do not follow, many more which I would question and many that, even if it were safe, I should not dare to profess for reasons of conscience."[8] Yet Erasmian reform did strike deep, it did seek change, it did challenge much within the established order. In this sense Erasmus occupied a middle ground in the controversy. As a result neither side could see him as their own, and both extremes viewed him as faithless and disloyal. The attacks that now befell Erasmus at least had this seemingly ambiguous centrality of his position at their base. And as the schism deepened and widened Erasmus stubbornly maintained his middle ground, at once faithful to his reform ideas, solicitous of the unity of the Church, and conciliatory in the face of the division that had come. He was an anomaly in an age of feverish polarization.

Part of the explanation for Erasmus's peculiar position—his moderation or middle ground or seeming ambiguity—probably lies deep within his personality. He looked at the world with a certain detachment and with something of a skeptical gaze; he was acutely sensitive to the self-deception and hypocrisy that abound; he was not given to scholastic definition or magisterial pronouncement; his language does at times seem cautiously qualified and uncertain—*oratio peregrina* I believe it has been called; he sensed by nature, I think, the frequent complexity and obscurity of the human situation. The Silenus figure whose outward appearance is quite different from its inward reality had deep attraction for him, and irony in one instance, tolerance in another, were the qualities that came most natural to him. This temper of mind or disposition, it seems to me, was reinforced by the kind and quality of his religious faith, just as that faith itself was influenced and formed by his natural inclinations. He saw charity as the great Christian virtue and peace and unity among Christians as its most cherished fruit. His "philosophy of Christ" was a practical guide, and it would lead men restored in Christ to the practice of charity and the haven of peace. Assertion or dogmatism, bitterness or hostility, party or strife were not of its essence and indeed were antithetical to the whole spirit and message of the Gospel. These particular emphases of Erasmus's religious faith, I have said, conformed to the natural bent of his mind, and the personal union thus effected contrived to disassociate him from all factionalism or fanaticism. Erasmus, it was said even in his own day, was "for himself," but in reality he stood, as he gazed out upon the follies of the world, for the Gospel of unity and peace. His moderation or middle ground was rooted in part at least in this equation. By the same token it was difficult for men of other tempers and other convictions to understand or accept him.

Erasmus thus presents certain special problems of comprehension and interpretation by virtue of his role or position in the schism, his message, and his personality. I do not intend to probe these factors in themselves any further. I have given my own brief statement and appraisal of them by way of background to what I now shall speak about. Controlling much of the opinion and controversy about Erasmus in his own day, they bear on the subsequent judgment and evaluation of him. Let us now come down to more recent times and see how some modern historians

have appraised the man. In that way we shall carry out our task
of describing Erasmus's place in history.

*   *   *

Let us begin with the biography of Erasmus by Preserved Smith
which I referred to at the beginning of my talk. The late Cornell
professor first published his work in 1923, and it was perhaps the
fullest and most scholarly study of Erasmus published in America
up to that time. It is still a very accessible book, having been reprinted as a paperback in 1962. Smith has given us a solid historical account of the great humanist's life, somewhat pedantic
and a little archaic in its style, but substantial, full of detail, and
not without present value. The Erasmus that emerges from his
pages is essentially the champion of rational Christianity, an
Erasmus "more skeptical and enlightened than most of his contemporaries." [9] It was not the scoffing rationalism that some have
claimed, according to Smith, but one that struck out at the super-
stitious and credulous, saw religion as an ethical concern, and
sought to rid it of its dogma. Indeed Erasmus's rational Christianity was primarily an undogmatic Christianity, and this, he de-
clares, was one of the main reasons why Erasmus broke with
Luther and the Protestants. [10] Reason and dogma it would seem
were the great incompatibles, their tension the essence of Erasmus's story. Smith deplored the fact that Erasmus did not support
the Reformation. "Convinced as I am that the Reformation was
fundamentally a progressive movement," he wrote, "the culmina-
tion of the Renaissance, and above all the logical outcome of the
teachings of Erasmus himself, I cannot but regard his later rejection of it as a mistake in itself and as a misfortune to the cause
of liberalism." [11] Nevertheless, Smith believed that Erasmus's efforts in "rationalizing religion" presaged and helped prepare the
enlightened future. [12] He was, in Smith's words, "the forerunner
and exponent of that type of Christianity at present prevalent
among large circles of our cultivated classes."

Smith's presentation of Erasmus as a rationalist heralding the
Enlightenment and the Liberal Age is, or at least was, a common
view. Derived from an earlier and cruder image of Erasmus as the
Voltaire of the sixteenth century, it concentrated on his satiric
thrusts at superstition and on his critical approach both as

scholar and as observer of the human scene. It appears to have been a fairly characteristic view in the nineteenth and early twentieth centuries, being congenial to the more cultivated middle-class *weltanschauung* of that era.[13] Nor is it entirely without its more recent versions. I am thinking chiefly of the thesis presented by H. A. Enno van Gelder in *The Two Reformations in the Sixteenth Century,* a work published at The Hague in 1961. Van Gelder sees Erasmus and the humanists inaugurating a more radical change in men's religious ideas than Luther and the Protestants. The latter still held to the traditional concept of Christianity as a doctrine of salvation, of man's redemption through Christ; the former shifted the whole emphasis, the whole orientation, to the moral or ethical sphere. For Erasmus, Van Gelder tells us, religion was "a doctrine of life instead of a mysterious redemption," and his view and mode of thinking are like that of the later rationalists.[14]

I must confess that such interpretations today have a rather old-fashioned ring to my ears. The product of less complicated times, they embody a perspective that not only is outmoded, but one that rests on very dated cultural preconceptions. They tend to reduce Erasmus, I am afraid, to the level of their own oversimplification. To some extent, I suppose, this is always inevitable, but in this instance it seems to me to be particularly unfortunate. There is so much more to Erasmus and his role in history than as a herald of rationalism or of ethical culture or as a precursor of the enlightened Christianity that Smith saw about him. I was particularly struck in reading Smith, despite the factual detail, by the incompleteness and narrowness of the portrait he gives. The deeper aspects of Erasmus's religion are hardly grasped, Erasmus's concern with the Fathers and the influence of that rich patristic heritage are scarcely treated, most surprisingly Erasmus's attitude and efforts toward conciliation and reunion in the face of schism are barely mentioned. In the light of this I am inclined to say that the whole relationship of Erasmus to the Reformation is misconceived and that the place in history Smith accords him is one that needs radical correction and relocation. Other historians, however, also have dealt with the problem. Let us see what their appraisal has been.

The year after Smith's work appeared the famous biography of Erasmus by the Dutch scholar and professor of history at Leyden Johann Huizinga was published. His book, not so ponderous or

documented as Smith's, is a more appealing study and is far more
sophisticated and nuanced in its characterization. The Erasmus of
Huizinga is not the champion of any great cause. He is the man
of letters and the theologian. His work was significant, his influence extensive, and many of his qualities—gentleness, moderation—are admirable, but he is not one of history's heroes. "Erasmus is the man who is too sensible and moderate for the heroic." [15]
Huizinga is particularly concerned with a personal analysis, and
his chapters on Erasmus's mind and character are the heart of his
book and its most interesting and controversial part. [16] The bent of
Erasmus's mind was ethical and esthetic, it sought freedom, clarity,
simplicity, it was acutely aware of the ambiguity of all things. But
"the world of his mind is imaginary," Huizinga tells us. "Erasmus
is never fully in contact with life." [17] Nor is his character without
its flaws: he tends to be self-centered, he is restless and discon-
tented, he is not straightforward or decisive. These qualities in
turn help explain Erasmus's role in the schism. It is "extremely
ambiguous." [18] He is not aware that his views are "no longer
purely Catholic," and he fails too to understand the great issues
and movements of his time. [19] This Erasmus, to whom Huizinga
attributes a "velvet softness" and whom he calls a "recluse," certainly stands in sharp contrast to the portrait of Smith. Not his
rationalism predominates, but his complex and withdrawn personality. Huizinga, I believe, is one of the first to focus so inten-
sively on the personality of the humanist reformer and to explain
so much in terms of its qualities and deficiencies. He has not gone
to the extreme of Erik Erikson in his psychoanalysis of the young
Luther, but he has, I believe, exaggerated the personal equation as
well as overemphasized certain features of that personality itself.
We could not give Erasmus too exalted a place in history on the
strength of Huizinga's recommendation.

Another and quite different Erasmus appears in the pages of a
study by the English scholar and writer Margaret Mann Phillips.
Her book, *Erasmus and the Northern Renaissance,* first published
in 1949, is an exceedingly well wrought and sympathetic essay. Mrs.
Phillips's Erasmus is the Christian humanist, the reformer, the man
of sincerity and humor and "refreshing common sense." In the face
of religious controversy and schism he is the apostle of "the middle
way," faithful to his original ideals, seeking and continuing to seek
a spiritual reform, but not the disruptive and intolerant reform of

the Protestants.[20] This "middle way" for Mrs. Phillips is not a matter of weakness or indecision, as Huizinga and others would have it, but a genuine position, a valid and consistent program in tune with Erasmus's fundamental spirit. It is his glory and his heritage. She writes:

That mellow, balanced sanity has always cast its spell, representing as it does the perfect work of the classical spirit tempered by the Christian ideal. It is indeed the middle way, not only between Catholic and Protestant, but between the mind and the heart. It needs on the one hand a liberated intellect, on the other a realization of the realms outside the reach of reason; a serene faith and a warm love of mankind are essentials to it. It is the climate of the mind in which humour grows, friendship blossoms and tolerance cultivates the flowers of the spirit: a tolerance resulting not from indolence but from decision and clear thinking.[21]

A third Erasmus thus arises—neither the champion of a rationalistic Christianity, nor the befuddled and indecisive spectator on life's drama, but the authentic Christian scholar and reformer pursuing a balanced middle course with clarity and consistency. A similar appraisal is given us in the very recent biography, published earlier this year, by the noted American Reformation scholar Roland H. Bainton, a work well titled *Erasmus of Christendom*. Bainton doesn't center his book, as Mrs. Phillips does, on the "middle way" theme, but he does present a moderate Erasmus, a man who cherished peace and concord, a man of piety and learning and deep religious purpose. The emphatic note struck by Bainton is the "inwardness" of Erasmus's religion. Erasmus sought above all to spiritualize religious life and practice—to turn it from the outward forms and ceremonials to an inward faith and dedication.[22] The spirit and the fruits of the spirit were what really mattered in the Christian dispensation.

In his preface Bainton tells us that Erasmus has not had his due on the score of interpretation. "Rejected by the Catholics as subversive and by the Protestants as evasive he has fallen chiefly into the hands of the rationalists who have appreciated him chiefly for his satire on contemporary superstitions."[23] Bainton intends to correct the image, and he does so, like Mrs. Phillips, by stressing the character and depth of Erasmus's religious thought and the seriousness of his Christian purpose. Though the work unfortunately is slightly flawed by a few annoying minor errors, Bainton's portrait, I believe, is more accurate than either Smith's or Huizinga's. There is, however, one aspect of Bainton's interpretation—and of Mrs. Phillip's too—that I should like to comment on. This is the explanation or view of Erasmus's relation to the Catholic Church. If for Smith Erasmus is actually a kind of liberal Protestant, for Bainton he is a liberal Catholic, indeed "the protagonist of liberal Catholic reform."[24] (In one place Bainton calls him "a precursor of the Counter-reformation."[25]) Yet the relationship between Erasmus and Catholicism, its authority, its tradition, its reform, is not well explored.[26] Bainton does not deny that Erasmus was and remained a Catholic, but the emphasis he places on Erasmus's spiritualizing tendencies and the conclusions he draws therefrom produce, it seems to me, a Sacramentarian or Schwenkfeldian Erasmus who is not really Catholic at all. A line may run from Erasmus in that direction, as Bainton says, but the fact is that Erasmus stayed in the Church and apparently believed in it. I was left somewhat confused, I must confess, by this aspect of Bainton's otherwise very probing and enlightening study.

I admit the question is a difficult one—Erasmus tends to elude conventional classification—but it is an important one, and it deserves very careful and discerning treatment. It is of considerable historical moment to know whether Erasmus's thought and spirituality and purpose were authentically Catholic or not and to what extent they relate to tradition and to the needs of the then contemporary Church. The question, of course, has not exactly been neglected. My point is that a good many of the analyses and appraisals of Erasmus on this score that I have seen seem to me either very vague and confusing or, if I may say so, quite shallow and uninformed. I have never been able to understand, for example, what Huizinga means when he keeps insisting that Erasmus's creed and concept of the Church were "no longer purely Catholic."[27] I do understand what Joseph Lortz means when, judging Erasmus from a Catholic point of view, he characterizes Erasmus's thought as "cultural religiosity," but in that case I believe the description is erroneous.[28] With regard to Mrs. Phillips's portrait of Erasmus with its emphasis on his "middle way," there is the tendency to locate Erasmus "between Catholic and Protestant." Perhaps this is meant to be understood loosely in the sense that

Erasmus stood between two warring camps, but the designation, I think, is a bit misleading. She does not adequately clarify this crucial relationship.[29] Perhaps one can't—or at least, perhaps, one can't make the neat, decisive clarification I seem to demand. Perhaps Erasmus's spirituality and moderate position are actually in between. The suggestion of that in Mrs. Phillip's essay calls to mind the more extensive interpretation of the great French Erasmian scholar Augustin Renaudet, and her book reflects in this regard, it would seem, the view of the former professor at the Collège de France. Let us now turn to his analysis and appraisal as we continue our survey.

One of Renaudet's chief works is his *Etudes érasmiennes,* published in Paris in 1939. It is a very detailed study of Erasmus's writings and thought during the critical years at Basel from 1521 to 1529. Renaudet's dominant theme is what he calls Erasmus's *modernisme.* Borrowing a term that had been applied to a movement within the Catholic Church at the turn of the twentieth century—a movement which stressed the historical evolution and relativity of doctrine and which had been formally condemned by Rome in 1907—Renaudet applies it to Erasmus's Biblical humanism and religious thought.[30] It is a slightly prejudicial label, to say the least. He views Erasmus's Christianity as "a religion of pure spirit," undogmatic and ethical, breaking sharply with theological tradition and orthodox formulation. Renaudet's approach associates him with the rationalist school of interpretation, but his appreciation and analysis of Erasmus's religion, it must be said, are both deeper and more sophisticated. A profounder Erasmus emerges from the pages of his careful study. He sees, however, the so-called *modernisme* of Erasmus as neither Protestant nor Catholic, as identifiable with neither the religion of Wittenberg and Zurich nor with that of Rome.[31] Erasmus is "between Roman conservatism and Lutheran revolution."[32] In a later book, *Erasme et l'Italie,* published in Geneva in 1954, Renaudet employed another memorable term to categorize Erasmus's position with respect to the rival Churches. The great humanist wanted, he tells us, a "troisième Eglise," a third Church.[33] This would be the Roman Church "profoundly reformed, renewed, modernized," but it is a Church which Renaudet by definition and explanation does not identify with the existing Catholic Church. It obviously is the ideal

Church of Erasmian *modernisme,* though it is interesting to note that in *Erasme et l'Italie* Renaudet has replaced the latter designation by the term and concept of a "troisième Eglise."

In both instances, but particularly in support of his thesis that Erasmus sought a third Church, Renaudet makes use of a very interesting quotation from the humanist's *Hyperaspistes* of 1526.[34] Writing in response to Luther following the latter's attack on him in *De servo arbitrio,* Erasmus said: "I will bear with this Church [meaning the Catholic Church] until I see a better one." Renaudet interprets this as substantiating his general theme, and it becomes a text for introducing the Erasmus of the third Church, of the middle way. There are difficulties, however, in using the *Hyperaspistes* quotation in this way. Jean-Claude Margolin, for one, takes issue with the meaning Renaudet has drawn from it and indeed with the whole interpretation in this regard of Renaudet. We might now turn to examine his view of Erasmus.

Margolin is a professor at Tours and the author of several recent studies in this field. The book I shall speak about is a general sketch or portrait of Erasmus, entitled *Erasme par lui-même,* published in Paris in 1965. Margolin gives us a scholarly, sensitive Erasmus whose Christianity is fully Catholic and whose religious thought embraces two fundamental principles: the spirit of liberty and the spirit of charity.[35] It is, Margolin tells us, "an immense commentary on the saying of St. Augustine: 'Love and do as you will,' " and it is "perfectly orthodox, since it proceeds essentially from the Gospel."[36] With regard to the *Hyperaspistes* quotation his view is that the full text does not permit Renaudet's interpretation.[37] In fact it actually affirms Erasmus's attachment or fidelity to the Catholic Church. It is prefaced by the clear statement, "I have never defected from the Catholic Church," and the complete sentence so cherished by Renaudet reads "I will bear with this Church until I see a better one, and it must bear with me until I become better." I might add that on the basis of the complete sentence we might develop the thesis of a second Erasmus.

Margolin is at paints to insist that he seeks and attempts to describe the authentic Erasmus whose true face has too often been hidden by partisan interpretation and by the *quod erat demonstrandum* of those who have dealt with him. I must confess that I share his attitude. Despite the real difficulties of understanding this complex personality and this incredibly prolific scholar and author, he has been wrenched too often by the one-sided perspectives and preconceived ideas of the historians who have portrayed him. He has continued to be in a sense the victim of polarization, of confessionalism, and of prejudice. The most serious distortion perhaps, I think, has been that of the rationalists who have been the least able to understand what he wrote and taught and sought to achieve. Nor have they been able, it would seem, even to start in that direction. It is almost inconceivable, for instance, that Preserved Smith should dismiss the great mass of his patristic work and scholarship and the integral role it had in his thought and program in a few pages in his chapter on Erasmus's "miscellaneous writings." Happily, that situation has been and is being rectified, but, as Bainton has well pointed out, Erasmus in the past has not had his due.

The image then of a profoundly Christian Erasmus fully orthodox and Catholic has gradually emerged. And let me say that on the basis of my own studies and judgment and frame of reference it is the image of the great humanist reformer that I see as I try to understand his work and his role in the troubled age in which he lived. The view of Margolin, of course, is neither the first nor the only interpretation of Erasmus along this line. Two other contemporary French scholars have given us a comparable judgment based on an even more precise analysis of Erasmus's theological orientation. I refer to Louis Bouyer of the French Oratory and to the Jesuit Henri de Lubac, professor of theology at Lyons. Both men have written extensively, and their works that bear most fully in this instance on our theme are Bouyer's *Autour d'Erasme,* published in Paris in 1955 and later translated and published here as *Erasmus and His Times,* and the fourth volume of de Lubac's magisterial *Exégèse médiévale* published in Paris in 1964.[38] Both of these scholars insist on Erasmus's fidelity to the patristic tradition and they stress the significance of his scholarly endeavor to reform and renew theology through a return to Scripture and the Fathers. It was the foundation of his whole reform program, the main source of his spirituality and life's work. Both examine at some length the modernist or "third Church" thesis of Renaudet and reject it, and they view Erasmus's thought and purpose as being in perfect conformity with Catholic doctrine and Catholic tradition. He may stand in sharp contrast to the scholasticism of the late Middle Ages, but that in itself does not place him beyond the pale of orthodoxy or qualify his essential Catholic faith. In fact, as Catholic theologians themselves they seem to hail the historic endeavor and achievement of Erasmus. Bouyer tells us that "his humanism reopened widely the permanent sources of Christian teaching" and that "this man who symbolizes better than anyone the renewal of the world . . . performed at the same time the function of its Christian conscience." [39] De Lubac, having considered the checkered course of Erasmus interpretation in the later part of his analysis, finally concludes with several texts from the letters of Thomas More defending and praising the noble work and virtue of his friend. "Nor surely can the faith of Erasmus be obscure," More wrote, "a faith adorned by so many labors, so many vigils, so many dangers, so many troubles, all sustained for the sake of Sacred Letters, the very storehouse of faith." [40]

This may be a suitable point at which to end. We have returned at length to the judgment of a man who knew Erasmus intimately in his own time and who shared so many of his scholarly concerns and plans and ideals with him. More's appraisal at least must be given great weight, and it points in a direction quite different than that taken by many latter interpreters of Erasmus and his role. We could, of course, continue with our survey of recent historians who have dealt extensively with Erasmus, for the number is large and their work significant, but I trust I have already given a fair indication of the modern approaches to Erasmus and of the problem of understanding him and assigning him his place in history.

The Place of Erasmus Today

By R. J. Schoeck

Richard J. Schoeck, distinguished professor of English at St. Michael's College of the University of Toronto, began his studies at McGill University before transferring to Princeton University where he received an M.A. and Ph.D. In addition to St. Michael's College, he has taught at Cornell University (1949–1955), the University of Notre Dame (1955–1961) and Princeton University (1964). Since 1963, he has also been professor of vernacular literature at the Pontifical Institute of Mediaeval Studies within the University of Toronto. Recognized as an eminent textual authority, Dr. Schoeck has served as a contributing editor for the *Well's Manual of Writings in Middle English* (1955—), *Neo-Latin News* (1955–1963), the St. Thomas More Project (1960—), and the Patterns and Literary Criticism series of the Universities of Toronto and Chicago (1962—). More recently, he has been appointed the general editor of an English edition of Erasmus's works, which will be published by the University of Toronto. His most noteworthy publications include: *Chaucer Criticism* (Notre Dame University Press, 1960–61), *Editing Sixteenth Century Texts* (University of Toronto Press, 1966) and *Style, Rhetoric and Rhythm: Essays by M. W. Croll* (Princeton University Press, 1966). He has also been a frequent contributor to *Mediaeval Studies* and *Studies in Philology*. These and other scholarly attainments have earned for him a number of fellowships and grants-in-aid from the American Council of Learned Societies, the Association for the Advancement of Education, the Canadian Council, the Guggenheim Memorial Foundation, and UNESCO. Furthermore, he was elected a life fellow by the Royal Historical Society and the Royal Society of Canada.

I want to begin with a little fable that has a bearing on Erasmus, and perhaps for all educators today:

> . . . he cast himself a rôle
> that needed ancestors and children to play;
> behind / ahead; dragon slaying dragon.
> Folly is more acceptable if played
> half by memory / half expectation /
> and violence loses unreality.[1]

And to build towards what the epigraph carries as a burden of meaning for me, I start from two positions already prepared: the first in a paper on "Erasmus and His Place in History" by John C. Olin, and the second in my own paper on "Erasmus and the Renaissance Re-discovery of Tradition" (in the Folger Symposium on Erasmus, 22 November[2]), for this is at least the tenth and perhaps culminating Erasmus celebration in what is after all only a probable centennial year.[3]

Erasmus has been much dealt with in 1969 (with one more symposium to come in 1970), and we might reflect on the sheer bulk of scholarly industry. The current literature on Erasmus is a formidable mass: in the fourteen years from 1936 to 1949, nearly 1,200 items; in the twelve years from 1950 to 1961 (reflecting the World War II drop off of research), more than 500;[4] since 1961, a marked acceleration in published research.

What has been the evaluation, the picture of Erasmus in all of this? As would be expected, he has always been the target of extremists on both sides. In his own *Compendium vitae* of early 1524 (when he was about 55), he himself tells us that "the Lutheran tragedy had burdened him with unbearable ill will" and that "he was torn apart by each faction, while he sought to serve the best interests of each." And in the same year he wrote to John Fisher, the holy and learned bishop of Rochester who was a good friend of Erasmus as he was of More: "Indeed, I war on three fronts: against these pagan Romans, who are meanly jealous of me; against certain theologians and friars, who use every stone at hand to bring me down; against some rabid Lutherans, who snarl at me because—so they say—I alone delay their own triumphs."[5] And he saw still another dimension in his role: "I am a Ghibelline for

the Guelphs, and a Guelph for the Ghibellines." [6] Little wonder
that the problem of evaluating Erasmus's place in history continues to be so complex, as Olin has already shown. Preserved
Smith (in 1923) viewed Erasmus as a rationalist heralding the
Enlightenment and the Liberal Age, and Van Gelder has largely
continued in that view. Huizinga presented a most attractive and
influential view in 1924 of Erasmus as anti-hero: not the champion
of any great cause, he was "the man who is too sensible and moderate for the heroic." In 1949, Margaret Mann Phillips enlarged
that view to offer a man of sincerity and humor and common sense,
a Christian humanist and reformer, but who followed a middle
way between Catholic and Protestant, between the mind and the
heart. There have been many others, obviously, and we can men-
tion but one further interpretation: Renaudet in his *Etudes érasmiennes* (1939) had concentrated upon the crucial Basel years
from 1521 to 1529 and applied to Erasmus's Biblical and religious
thought the term *modernisme* which he borrowed from the stormy
early twentieth-century movement; and in 1954 in *Erasme et
l'Italie* Renaudet developed this earlier view of Erasmus into a
thesis that claimed him as wanting a *troisième Eglise,* the Roman
Church "profoundly reformed, renewed, modernized"; and for this
he based much upon Erasmus's own statement that, "I will bear
with this Church [meaning the Roman Catholic Church] until I see
a better one." But Margolin and Olin have since challenged that
part of Renaudet's thesis and have stressed the fact that the crucial
statement just quoted is prefaced by Erasmus's declaration: "I
have never defected from the Catholic Church"; for Renaudet
failed to complete the full original sentence, which should go on
to read: "I will bear with this Church until I see a better one, and
it must bear with me until I become better." More and more
scholars are reading all of Erasmus, and what has been emerging
in Erasmian scholarship of recent years—and here we are laid
under debt to the work of Bataillon, Bouyer, de Lubac especially—
is the image of an Erasmus who was fully orthodox (let us not
forget that he died before Trent began, so that we do not try to
make him conform to the defensive orthodoxies of Trent), deeply
religious (in his fashion), fully committed. He was faithful to the
patristic tradition (and we can never forget how large a part of
his working life was devoted to the editing of St. Jerome and a
number of other Church Fathers); he never lost sight of the cen-

trality of the Scriptures to the Christian life (for he regarded his editing of the New Testament and the writing of the Paraphrases as his major life-work; and the balance and humanity of his *philosophia Christi* give us the main thrust of nearly all of his popular writings. We can here take the testimony of his good friend Thomas More in this light, and no other: "Nor surely," More wrote, "can the faith of Erasmus be obscure, a faith adorned by so many labors, so many vigils, so many dangers, so many troubles, all sustained for the sake of Sacred Letters, the very storehouse of faith." And so it seems to me that Erasmian studies of the 1970s are going to deepen our understanding of the interrelationship of theological and scriptural studies with his humanism. In my own recent Folger lecture I endeavored to establish that Erasmus's sense of tradition as a living dynamic was consistent in theology, law, scripture studies, and literature; and I shall return to his rediscovery of tradition in my conclusion.

In point of fact, we have begun to walk all the way around the traditional literary or historical view of Erasmus and to see it more nearly in the round. We are beginning to recognize that he was no skeptic, no rationalist; that he was not (as one wit would have him) a descendant of a long line of maiden aunts, for he was *engagé* and tough: a humanist and a man in holy orders, he could ask of a Benedictine abbot (one Paul Volz), "for what is the city but a monastery"? (And I would suggest that such a question was no less revolutionary in 1518 than it would be in 1969, if addressed to any administrator of a Catholic institution in an inner city of North America.)[7]

He may well be regarded as an ancestor of the intellectual *clerc,* in the sense of Julien Benda, whose descendants no longer kept up the fight, of whose *trahison* Benda could write so persuasively[8] —indeed, it is worth recalling that Benda calls Erasmus (with Goethe and a few others) one who was a great patrician of the mind. Beyond observing that linguistically *tradition* and *trahison* are cognate, and that an *Überblick* of western culture could find countless examples of tradition that became betrayal, when it was either handed over to the enemy without a fight to keep it alive or put into so guarded and fortified a position that it petrified and thus became only a relic of real tradition—beyond observing, then, that there are many ways to betray tradition—I would nail up to the wall the thesis, some day to discuss and defend, that it is the special responsibility of us *clercs* to keep tradition alive.

What I have been doing for the past few minutes, is nothing less than an exercise in tradition. One begins by questioning what is essential and viable, but one cannot end there. One works (especially if he is a teacher of humanities) towards transmittal, through his students who will in turn question and carry on; but he must himself have begun by questioning and have continued by evaluating—provisionally, to be sure, but with serious commitment.

First we mark Erasmus as a man whose work is today condemned to fragmentation, for we are compelled to read it in separated contexts and unrelated approaches; a man who becomes—as the burden of the past tends to harden inherited views and judgments of him by scholars whose sense of the whole of past tradition tends to diminish—a man who becomes, that is to say, progressively more difficult to understand. Even the commendable essay by Olin attempting to put Erasmus into a place in history suffers from a departmentalized approach: it is the judgment only of previous historians, and it proceeds only by the conventional techniques of historians. With Huizinga we do have a widening of the nets: they are woven with different strands, and they are cast more widely; but it is not until Bouyer and de Lubac begin to relate theology with scripture, and secondarily humanism, that the larger whole of Erasmus begins to emerge. There are gains from specialization, but we pay a high price for those gains: a point which I think needs our patient study and very full reflection. Erasmus stands above both the departmentalization of modern history and the problematics of a modern Benda, yet in the modern university we contribute to misunderstanding by setting up walls to prevent the reading of Erasmus's writings as a whole.

How many graduate students in English have read more than the *Praise of Folly* (and that in translation, of course)? This is no dilletantish point, for unless one follows—what weak translations cannot give—the subtle gradation of tone which structures the irony, to move ultimately to the folly of Christ, one misses much.

How many graduate students in French, who read Rabelais, have dug into the Erasmian roots of Rabelais's thought on marriage and scripture?[9]

In scripture studies today very little attention is paid to sixteenth-century work in Scripture, yet how much of the force and the directions of Reformation movements can be understood without an understanding of how they read the Bible? How many have read all of the preface to the New Testament, and the enlarged *Paraclesis?*

How many theologians have read that profound work, *Ratio Verae Theologiae?* Or preachers, the *Paraclesis;* or historians of ecclesiastical institutions the hint on monastery/city in the prefatory letter to Volz?

Historians of education will refer to the *Education of a Christian Prince,* and the *Ciceronianus* is printed in the series of a teachers' college; but how many educational historians relate these significantly to Erasmus's humanism, and to the profound influence in the history of education of the *Colloquies* and *Adages?*

One could go on, but I trust that my point has been made. At a time when scholars are beginning to walk around the statue of Erasmus and to see it in toto, their students are allowed to view it from one departmental window only.

Yet the historical importance of Erasmus is well-nigh incalculable. I cannot think of his counterpart in the history of modern European thought and letters—not even Voltaire, whose philosophical influence was perhaps greater, but his literary influence surely less, and whose range is simply not anything like that of Erasmus. There have been something like 2,000 editions of Erasmus's works, among which we must stress the *New Testament* and the *Adagia,* each of which in the sixteenth century passed through nearly a hundred authorized and unauthorized editions; and these were widely scattered in the Low Countries, France, and Switzerland especially (much less so in Italy, or Spain)—but even these data do not fully or accurately measure his influence, for there were many translations, adaptations, borrowings, attacks and replies, and a still wider indirect influence.

Let us ask whether departmental structures do not need scrutiny when we are confronted with the fact of our neglect of so great a writer. Given the accident of his birth—a real accident—we cannot leave Erasmus to that rarest of Phoenixes, a department of Nederlandsche literature. We should insure that an occasional course in Erasmus will make his thought and writings *as a whole,* in a body, available to specialists from literature, theology, history, etc. I would not argue against departmental structures (provided that there is flexibility), for they are needed for discipline; and we must grant that there can be only a smattering and scattering of ignorance in a student who has "done" all Western Civilization in two years—*grant?* indeed, we *must* assume it, both in such an undergraduate and perhaps also in his instructor. But we cannot be absolute; there must also be provisions at both the undergraduate and the graduate levels for inter- and trans-disciplinary work. This has been a digression, but it is a needed one: both for the present subject, and for the present-day considerations of roles, functions, and structures of the modern university.

I return then to the place of Erasmus today, and for this I would draw avowedly upon my own Folger paper.

To speak in large terms, the age of Erasmus was one in which tradition had hardened: in the universities at the end of the fifteenth century, scholastic curricula were deeply intrenched and textbooks were, by and large, centuries old. Witness More's trenchant *caveat* that "a conviction that is first handed on by stupid teachers and then strengthened in the course of years is extremely capable of perverting the judgment of even sound minds." [10] Hence the well-nigh universal attack by humanists on scholastic logic, in fact upon a wide swath of medieval habits of thought—More in his *Utopia,* Rabelais—the list would grow quickly. In areas of faith and belief, the fierce wars on heresy had won patterns and modes of conformity by 1500, but at a great expense both of institutional freedom (witness the lamentable state of things in late fifteenth-century Oxford) and of individual conscience. Pico's fresh, and dangerous, enthusiasm for the freedom of the individual must be seen in this context, as well as Thomas More's fight for the freedom of individual conscience, extolled in Roper's saints-life of a lawyer with a superlatively developed conscience; and the entire career of Erasmus, I urge, must be viewed. For in an era in which tradition had long hardened, Erasmus fought for a sense of freedom, of development, of the possibility of organic change: nearly every book of his is a sign of it, for Erasmus was the first master of the growing book, and the prime example is the *Adagia* with many editions that not only multiplied adages (818 proverbs in 1500 grows to 3,260 in 1508, and these grew and were regrouped again in 1515, 1520, 1523, 1526, 1528, and 1533) but also developed the thought—as Erasmus wrote in a 1523 letter:

Well, just as we spend our life seeking to make ourselves better, so we shall not cease to make our writings richer and more accurate until we ourselves cease to live.[11]

Like More, and alongside More, Erasmus defended humanism against the attack of narrow-minded young theologians like Dorp, of ossified institutions like the faculty of theology at the University of Paris, of calcified disciplines like logic and dialectic; and the position defended against Dorp and others (in massive epistles, apologia, and other writings) is consistent with the position of the *Ratio Verae Theologiae,* the Preface to his New Testament of 1516, which was expanded and published separately in 1519. One finds worked out in the *Ratio* what Erasmus had put as a question in the *Enchiridion:*

> Quid igitur faciet Christianus?
> Negliget ecclesiae mandata? contemnet
> honestas maiorum traditiones? damnabit
> pias consuetudines? Immo si informus
> est, servabit ut necessarias, sin firmus
> et perfectus. . . .[12]

For the Erasmian position on tradition is everywhere consistent, namely, that there is a *consensus omnium,* a living and growing body which the individual must approach humbly, through study, and to which he then gives his individual acceptance or assent: that is, there is an obligation, but there must be the self-giving.[13]

I have already spoken of the closeness of More and Erasmus in the early years, and their collaborative friendship needs no emphasis today. But here I would contrast the More of the 1520s and early 1530s—that is, the More in his forties and fifties—in order to give a measure of Erasmus's essential balance and consistency.

I ask you to look not at the author of the early poems, the translator of epigrams and the life of Pico, or the author of the *Utopia,* but the later More, during his years from about 45 to his death at 58. And looking at the More of the polemical works, I am led to ask this question: "How are we to understand or judge the sense of tradition, of living tradition, in a man who in his *Responsio ad Lutherum* attacked Luther so uniformly and totally, so rigor-ously—I would say, indeed, savagely—finding nothing to praise and apparently nothing to take up for consideration in the reform of the Church?" To ask such a question is to look for factors that could explain the widening gap between More and Erasmus in this area—I repeat, *in this area,* for in so many other areas More would have been as consistent as Erasmus and the two would have enjoyed a continuation, *mutatis mutandis,* of their intimate and cooperative relationship.

Thomas More was about 46 in 1523, the year which I take to delineate the change, but he had been unofficially in the King's service half a dozen years, unofficially nearly ten since his trade mission to the Low Countries in 1515. More's election as Speaker of Parliament in 1523 further underscores his ambiguous position (his growing involvement in public policy, both publicly and psychologically); for although More was a spokesman for parliament (and his address in 1523 is a noble document in the history of freedom of speech), he had of course been a member of the King's Council since 1517–18, and under-treasurer and knight since 1521.

I would here emphasize the probability that More seems to have been drawn into the examination of heretics in some official or quasi-official capacity quite early in his public career, perhaps by virtue of his office as under-sheriff of London (which he was from September 3, 1510, onward); but certainly he was deeply enough involved, as I have shown elsewhere,[14] in the celebrated affair of Richard Hunne, which lasted from 1511 until Hunne's death in 1514, and his posthumous burning as a heretic, and continued to figure in the Standish-Kidderminister debate over Criminous Clerks in 1515, which occupied parliament, the King's Council, and many of the learned common and canon lawyers of England throughout 1515; it then rose again to the surface of polemics in 1529, and More tried to defend both canon law and the handling by the hierarchy of the Hunne affair in his writings from 1529 to 1533. In More's *Dialogue Concerning Heresies, Confutation, Apology,* and *Debellation,* there is again and again indication of involvement in matters concerning heresy long before he became Lord Chancellor in 1529. I could not say at what point his primary judgment in this category became essentially legalistic, but I would insist that before 1523 (the date of the publication of the *Responsio*) he had begun to think this way. Let us recall too the moving anecdote in Roper's *Life of More:* of More's prayers for William Roper at the time of his son-in-law's commitment to

Lutheranism, probably just after his marriage to More's beloved daughter Margaret—which means that in 1521, or shortly afterward, Roper became a Lutheran but later returned to the Catholic faith. Given More's deep and special fondness for his daughter, this incident might help to explain his hatred of the influence of Lutheranism.

The fact remains that in 1523 his *Responsio* tries to counter Luther on every point—*tota in toto et tota in qualibet parte,* as C. S. Lewis comments:[15] "that the reader, whatever page he lights upon, should find there all that he needs for refutation of the enemy"; and it does so with extraordinary vulgarity (even for his times), and a total lack of charity. One example must suffice:

> But meanwhile, for as long as your reverend paternity will be determined to tell these shameless lies, others will be permitted, on behalf of his English majesty, to throw back into your paternity's shitty mouth, truly the shit-pool of all shit, all the muck and shit which your damnable rottenness has vomitted up, and to empty out all the sewers and privies onto your crown divested of the dignity of the priestly crown, against which no less than against the kingly crown you have determined to play the buffoon.[16]

More, it is abundantly clear, read Luther—or considered some of his teachings by second-hand information and report—as having no possible relation with the living development of Christian doctrine. An idea that is not orthdox was ipso facto to More heretical, and it must be condemned; this is the logic of More's rhetorical strategies, and the theological thrust is an ever greater insistence on more and more inclusive and explicit orthodoxy. The contrast with Erasmus is terribly obvious: "I speak of these things more freely," he could write in 1519 to Albert of Brandenburg, "because I am not involved in any way in the cause of Reuchlin and Luther." [17] And though he engaged in much controversy and debate in the 1520s, there is nothing I know of that stoops so low as More's *Responsio.*

The outbreak of peasant uprisings in the Schwarzwald during June, 1524—which spread quickly and widely through Swabia, Franconia, Thuringia, and into the Rhineland, and reports of which circulated in England with considerable exaggerations of the facts —for More, these events would have confirmed in the sphere of the political order his fears concerning the dangerous effects of Lutheranism.

Yet, even if all that I say concerning reasons for More's fierceness towards heretics be so, can we accept such fears as sufficient explanation for his violent reaction to Tyndale, Saint-German, and others from 1528 to 1533, in writings which I would characterize as theological overkill? From the date of the authorization by Tunstall, Bishop of London, for More to read Protestant books in order to refute them in English—March 7, 1528, and given so legal a mind as More's, a mind so alert to potential dangers, is it not possible that it might have been issued at More's request?— from 1528 to 1533, More wrote several thousand pages of polemics, in which there is but rarely the notion that anything from the reformers might conceivably be valid, might contribute to the desperately needed reform of the Church and Christian society (which he himself had proclaimed in *Utopia*). Indeed by the time of the *Debellation* (1533), the inescapable conclusion, it seems to me, is that tradition is no longer dynamic for More: it is now a repository which must be safeguarded. To use his own metaphor from greener days, it has become an established treasure, a deposit behind walls, which must be defended against the enemy—and it is worth considering the extent and force of military and paramilitary metaphors that run from the titles of the *Confutation* and *Debellation* and into the works themselves.

The contrast between More and Erasmus from 1517 to 1523 is striking enough, and it becomes the greater after 1523; and it would seem that Erasmus is not only trying to walk the middle of the road—and that metaphor, while superior to expressions of value-less neutrality, is really unsatisfactory. Erasmus was trying to keep the lines of communication open (as parents today speak of the efforts to stay in touch with, to continue to make meaningful contact with, the younger and sometimes militant generations). Erasmus was trying to preserve the possibilities of true dialogue, so beloved to generations of humanistic effort, so essential to their principles and values—but I have just written about reading the *Utopia* as dialogue and I don't want to subject my listeners to critical overkill. Even in theological debates like Erasmus's strenuous one with Dolet, there is nothing that approaches the vituperative violences of More's *Responsio*.[18]

On the crucial subject of heresy, Erasmus comes through admirably, and one could cite a number of passages in the letters, the *Paraclesis,* the *Ratio,* and elsewhere. But the letter to Albert of Brandenburg will serve again, and two brief passages must suffice:

Besides, while the proper task of theologians is to instruct, I now observe that many do nothing but constrain or destroy and extinguish, though Augustine, even in the case of the Donatists, who were not only heretics but also savage brigands, does not approve of those who only use force and do not instruct. Men, whom gentleness especially becomes, seem to thirst for nothing except human blood, and they eagerly desire only that Luther be seized and destroyed. But this is to play the part of the executioner, not the theologian. . . .

And, further:

At one time the heretic was heard respectfully, and he was absolved if he made amends; but if he persisted in his heresy after his conviction, the extreme penalty was his exclusion from communion with the Church. Now the crime of heresy is a different matter, and yet for any trifling reason the cry is immediately raised. . . . I admit that the charge of a corrupted faith is grave, but it is not necessary to turn everything into a question of faith. . . .[19]

Yet I would not want to oversimplify the complexities of history (nor to fail to recognize that More had responsibilities as Lord Chancellor which Erasmus as a private citizen did not); and one must recognize too that Erasmus's attitude changed significantly in 1520, both after the papal condemnations and still more, I think, after Luther's several treatises of that year. As Gilmore has formulated the situation:

He feared the consequences of what he now saw to be a revolution, and he deplored Luther's appeal to the general public. As the Lutheran movement took shape and the gap between Rome and Wittenberg widened, Erasmus's position became increasingly uncomfortable. . . .[20]

The *Inquisition de fide* (so ably edited by Craig Thompson) must indeed be read not only, or not simply, as a theological tract in its abstractive structure, but as a characteristically Erasmian effort "to explore in a dialogue the implications of the religious division." And there is a significant shift from this dialogic effort to the definition of position in his treatise on the freedom of the will, a shift from dialogue to tract, from exploration to separating definition. The *Hyperaspistes,* while they are of course elaborations of Erasmus's original argument, are also confessions that the possibility of dialogue is diminishing; here Erasmus moves closer to the polemic spirit and techniques of More.

But the dialogue spirit in Erasmus returns and continues in the late *Colloquies,* and it is in these that I would see one of the marks of Erasmus's greatness as humanist. For it is one thing to write dialogues in the halcyon years before 1516—that was a time for summer humanists—it is quite another thing to write dialogues as Erasmus did in the winter years from 1522 to 1534. One must recognize, nay celebrate, the greatness of More's achievement in the *Dialogue of Comfort,* written during his imprisonment in the Tower, 1534–35; yet there is relatively little in this work to indicate any readiness on More's part to enter into dialogue with reformers. There is compassion, but only for his coreligionists, whom he foresaw as poised on the brink of disaster; the dialogue renders his towering powers of intellect and faith and will, but it does not engender fraternal charity towards the reformers. I would take nothing away from this great *consolatio*—one of the great works after Boethius in this genre that has its share of literary masterpieces—but there is nothing in it to change what I have said concerning More as against Erasmus on the point of tradition.

"Like all life," Curtius writes, "tradition is a vast passing away and renewal."[21] To the humanist scholar (and Richard Schlatter has spoken eloquently of his offices in a recent ACLS paper on "Humanist Scholarship in the U.S."), the gathering and preservation and evaluation of tradition have been a vital part of his whole effort, scarcely to be separated from his enjoyment of good letters. It is one of the responsibilities of the literary critic (to use the language and perception of F. O. Matthiessen),[22] continually to make the effort to repossess the past. For, as we have been shown by a number of critics beginning with Matthew Arnold—but new generations of students seem not to have learned the lesson—for his own work the critic has to be both involved in his age and detached from it. This double quality of experiencing our own time to the full and yet being able to weigh it in relation to other times is what the critic must strive for, if he is to be able to discern and demand the works of art that we need most.

> . . . he cast himself a rôle
> that needed ancestors and children to play;
> behind / ahead . . .

But our burden is still larger. Literature is but a part of the humanities, and I must speak of the burden of the teacher and scholar in the humanities, for it is here that Erasmus has still larger place today. Without its bases of tradition, mankind is like an individual without memory. "Memory is a dynamic principle," the great Russian critic Ivanov wrote, and he went on to remind that "forgetting is weariness and interruption of movement, descent and return to the condition of a relative inertness." [23] As it is with the individual man, so is it with a people or a race: a culture that turns its back upon tradition is forgetting and interrupting its organic movement. It is, however, a travesty of tradition to erect walls that halt movement, for tradition is not that which is safeguarded in a vault or behind barriers: for that would be to harden the thing which tradition is keeping alive into a doctrine that cannot long live by itself, into a fixed and unchallengeable choice of canonical books. Ironically enough, it was More, in an early writing, who used the figure of the locked chest at one point for such a concept. Living tradition is process, not product, and an imaginative transmittal of what has been inherited can always bring life, indeed is necessary to sustain institutional life.

The Thomas More who defended humanism then under attack in his celebrated 1517 letter to Oxford University—he knew this, as did the Erasmus who praised with such beautiful irony the folly that would destroy tradition and, with consummately managed gradation of tone, allows his irony to deepen and embrace the folly and simplicity of Christ and his followers. But after 1523 I would look to Erasmus for the one who kept viable a sense of tradition, not More. Let me read an extended passage from one of the adages which Erasmus added to the 1526 edition, for it is a splendid statement by Erasmus on the new and the old.[24]

On the other hand, if the older men were ready to accept (with civility and fairness) what are really not newcomers and strangers, but guests of old days returning to claim their right of citizenship, they would find the addition of these things was far from useless, and lets in new light not negligible at all. As it is, they wage irreconcilable war on old friends, as if they were enemies. They call "new" the things that are the oldest of all, and they call "old" what is really new. It is something new, [with boys who are to learn grammar] to stuff them with *modus significandi,* and read them crazy lists of words which teach nothing but to speak faultily. It is something new to accept a youth as a student in Philosophy, Law, Medicine or Theology, who can understand nothing in the ancient authors owing to his ignorance of the language they speak. It is something new, to exclude from the Holy of Holies of Theology anyone who has not sweated for years over Averröes and Aristotle. It is something new to stuff young men, who are reading for a degree in Philosophy, with Sophistical nonsense and fabricated problems, mere brain-teasers [meras ingeniorum cruces]. It is something new in the public teaching of the Schools, for the answers to differ according to the methods of Thomists or Scotists, Nominalists or Realists. It is something new to exclude any arguments which are brought from the sources of Holy Scripture, and only accept those which are taken from Aristotle, from the Decretals, from the determinations of the Schoolmen, from the glosses of the professors of papal law, or from precedents (inane for the most part) distorted from Roman law. If we are to be offended by what is new, these are the really new things. If we approve of what is old, the oldest things of all are what are being brought forward now. Unless, maybe, "new" means coming from the century of Origen, and "old" means what started up three hundred years ago and has gone from bad to worse ever since. The only course left to us now, therefore, is this: that the study of languages and of good letters, coming back to take their place amongst us and spring up again from the roots, as it were, should courteously and peaceably work their way into the company of those disciplines which have held sway for so many centuries in the universities, and without disparaging anyone's particular study, should be of use to the studies of all. . . . Let them warn, and help, and correct, [Erasmus concludes with an evocation of the Psalm that figures in the Office], as a conscientious maidservant warns, and helps, and corrects her mistress.

For us today there are a few final reflections. From the past, much remains—and can we blame young students who at times feel too much? Young artists, young citizens, young lovers who feel too heavily on their backs the burden of history, of all that is inherited? Yet it is the continuing task of the historical critic to study that past, continuously to reevaluate it (let us admit that we must resolve to do this more rigorously than we have done in practice), to test its relevance to our own values and needs, but remembering that such a test is always only provisional, only a moment or stage in an ever-changing development. Therefore as humanist (I return to modify our epigraph), each should cast himself a role that needs ancestors and children to play; behind / ahead. . . . One last thing: as perhaps the greatest of the great humanists of the Renaissance, Erasmus never lost sight either of the essentiality of enjoyment as part of the process in or of relevance to the good life as the end of learning. If those new barbarians, our students, to whom we devote our lives as teachers, do not understand that tradition must always be rediscovered—and that it is worth the effort—then we shall have failed as teachers of the humanities. *Saint Erasmus,* we can indeed say with humanistic piety, *pray for us.*

Precatio Dominica

in Septem Portiones Distributa

by Desiderius Erasmus

(Basel: Johann Froben, 1523)

Translated into English

by Margaret More Roper

(London: Thomas Berthelet, c. 1525)

Diplomatic Reprint

edited by Richard L. DeMolen

Introduction

Since *A deuout treatise vpon the Pater noster . . .* , which reveals something of the meditative nature of Erasmus, was composed during an evolutionary stage in the English language and was translated from the Latin[1] by a daughter of Sir Thomas More, we feel it deserves greater scrutiny and wider circulation. Moreover, because it survives in only three known copies and has never been reprinted after ca. 1531, we offer it as the final contribution to this commemorative collection. Above all, one thing seems clear in the relationship between the author and the translator of the *Precatio Dominica:* they were mutual admirers. Following the birth of Margaret More Roper's first child in 1523, Erasmus dedicated his *Commentary on the Christmas Hymn of Prudentius* to her. Margaret responded generously to this honor by translating the following meditation and in the process sealed a lifelong friendship.

In works of biography, it has been customary to suggest that Erasmus of Rotterdam was more concerned with exegesis and the classics than with Christian meditation and prayer.[2] As the Prince of Humanists, he was supposedly caught up in the scholarly pursuits of the age and, therefore, had little time for religious devotion. Notwithstanding his humanistic orientation, certain biographers would also argue that Erasmus developed a philosophy of Christ—a way of life which chose Christ as its model but selectively deemphasized acts of Christian piety.[3] Somehow, Erasmus was able to equate humanism and Christianity but not Christianity and piety. It is of interest, therefore, to examine a treatise such as the *Precatio Dominica,* which was written at the very peak of Erasmus's career, and to judge his religious disposition and interior life in terms of its content. Those biographers who maintain the second of the above positions would expect to find a secularly oriented mind, a kind of text which reflected the vanities of a scholar, who had been laden with academic and courtly honors. But such is not the case. For Erasmus was a more devoted disciple of Christ than he was of human vice and folly. Highly reflective, the *Precatio Dominica* emphasizes a deeply devout, and often neglected, side of Erasmus's nature. Like the Brethren of the Common Life, who instructed him during his youth, Erasmus was a master of the art of Christian meditation. Taking leave of mundane preoccupations, he soared heavenward in search of a comforting and loving father. Indeed, only an exceptionally pious practitioner could have observed:

As often soeuer as for thy loue we despice and sette nought by the realme of this worlde/ and with full trust hange vpon the heuenly kyngdome/ that thou hast promysed vs: as often also/ as we forsake and leaue honourynge of erthely richesse/ and onely worshyp and embrace the precious and gostly lernyng of the gospel/ as often as we refuse those thynges/ . . . So often father thou warrest in vs/ and ouercomest the realme of the deuyll/ and openyst the myght and power of thy realme.

Yet, at the same time, the work also reveals one of Erasmus's principal faults: a form of religious anti-Semitism, rather than racial, which was shared by many contemporary humanists. With unkind disparity, he lashes out at the Jews of his own day in these words:

The iewes also neuer cesse in their sinagoges and resorte of people/ from dispitefull and abominable bacbytinge of thy onely sonne/ wherby in the meanetyme they sclaundre the/ sithe it can nat be chosen whan thy sonne is misfamed (whiche is the very clerenesse of thy glorie) but that infamy also must redounde in the.

But, then, was not this the real Erasmus? Like other men of his time, was he not a composite of virtue and vice; both a lover of Christ, whom he had never seen, and a hater of certain men's beliefs with whom he was in daily contact? Even so, his anti-Semitism appears all the more jarring in the face of the syncretism of more enlightened humanists. In the last analysis, we are especially fortunate to have record of this anomaly and to have had it expressed so poignantly in the garb of the *Precatio Dominica*.

Desiderius Erasmus first published his *Precatio Dominica* at the press of Johann Froben in 1523. Before the year was out, the work itself proved to be immensely popular and appeared in three Latin editions. By 1524, six Latin editions and two translations, one in

English and the other in German, were circulating in Europe. Eventually, according to the *Bibliotheca Erasmiana,* published by the Library of the State University of Ghent in 1893, twenty-seven separate editions of the *Precatio Dominica* were variously published between 1523 and 1861. In addition, ten more editions of this work have survived for which there are no dates of publication.

Margaret More Roper's translation of the *Precatio Dominica* appeared in four editions. Wynkyn de Worde, the Alsatian émigré and successor to Caxton, issued the first one in 1524.[4] Although this first edition is no longer extant, it seems likely that it was identical with those succeeding issues which were published by Thomas Berthelet and Robert Redman if for no other reason than the same printer's device and a paraphrase of the title have been identified as belonging to this edition. The surviving second edition appeared ca. 1525/1526 and bears the title, *A deuout treatise vpon the Pater noster.* . . .[5] Two known copies of this edition exist; one of them is in the British Museum, the other is to be found in the St. Thomas More Collection at Yale University. Still another issue was published ca. 1531.[5] The only known copy of this third edition is in the John Rylands Library.[7] Finally, Robert Redman published an undated fourth edition.[8] No copies of this issue have apparently survived.

Beneath the words on the title page of the surviving issues of Margaret's translation appears a woodcut (9.5 cm. x 5 cm.), within ornamental borders, of a woman, seated at a desk. Almost expressionless, the figure is turning the page of an open book.[9] On the reverse side of this leaf is a full-page woodcut (13 cm. x 9.2 cm.) of Thomas Cardinal Wolsey's coat of arms.[10] The title page device, which Berthelet used in 1525, appeared earlier in works published by Wynkyn de Worde.[11] No doubt Berthelet had purchased the device from de Worde for inclusion in later editions of the translation.

Preceding the text of the translation of the *Precatio Dominica* is a dedicatory letter written by Richard Hyrde (d. 1528) to a student of his, Frances Staverton. Dated October 1, 1524, the twelve-page letter lauds humanistic learning and especially the education of girls—a cause to which Hyrde was particularly devoted. Indeed, Foster Watson has asserted that Hyrde's letter is "the first reasoned claim of the Renascence period, written in English, for the higher education of women."[12] Master Hyrde was employed at this time as a tutor in the Chelsea household of Sir Thomas More.[13] His young charge was the daughter of More's oldest sister, Joan, and Richard Staverton, who served as one of the prenotaries in the Sheriff's Court of London.[14] Though Frances Staverton and Margaret More Roper were first cousins, it seems unlikely that Hyrde ever taught Margaret since she was apparently close to his age. The Lord Chancellor employed Hyrde as a tutor to his grandchildren because he enjoyed a reputation as a classical scholar and physician.[15] Almost nothing else is known about Hyrde except that he graduated B. A. from Oxford in 1519[16] and died of a fever in March of 1528.[17] It seems that Hyrde, who had accompanied Stephen Gardiner and John Foxe to Italy as Latin secretary on a mission from Cardinal Wolsey to Clement VII, had been overcome by a storm and soaked by a fall into a stream.[18]

Having enjoyed a reputation as a court tutor and defender of women's education, Richard Hyrde introduced the circle of English humanists to the youngest and ablest of the native female scholars, Margaret More Roper. She was the eldest daughter of Sir Thomas More and his first wife, Jane Colt. Brought up in the company of two sisters, one brother, and assorted relatives, Margaret achieved in her own lifetime a reputation for erudition and writing ability. Even an early marriage to William Roper in 1521 did not deter her from critical scholarship. Throughout her married life, she was a devoted wife and mother who succeeded in combining a love of learning with her domestic duties.[19]

By October 1, 1524, Margaret had completed her translation of the *Precatio Dominica*. The date of composition is established by Hyrde in his dedicatory letter. In it he asserts that Margaret's translation had already been completed before he composed his prefatory remarks to Frances Staverton. The translation itself is of significance for at least three reasons: it is the earliest translation by a young woman of nineteen on record; it is probably the best English prose translation from the Latin produced by a woman up to that time;[20] and finally, because of its superior qualities, the reader can be reasonably assured that Margaret's translation in its several editions helped to establish English as a literary language.[21] Her skill at turning graceful phrases and her choice of non-Latinized words appear all the more remarkable in an age experimenting with orthography and neologizing.

Textual Note

The following edition of Margaret More Roper's English translation of the *Precatio Dominica* by Desiderius Erasmus (Basel,
1523) is a diplomatic reprint in which certain contractions, such as
"&," "yᵉ," "yᵗ," "wᵗ," "pte," and "pfitable," have been silently expanded. The rarity of the work, together with its intrinsic value
as one of the earliest examples of an English translation from the
Latin, prompted the editor to keep as close as possible to the
original. The text for this reprint was based upon the ca. 1525/
1526 copy in the British Museum.

A deuout treatise vpon the Pater no-

ster/ made fyrst in latyn by the moost fa-

mous doctour mayster Erasmus

Roterodamus/ and tourned

into englishe by a yong

vertuous and well

lerned gentylwoman of .xix.

yere of age.

[by Margaret More Roper (1505–1544)]
London: Thomas Berthelet, ca. 1525

Richard Hyrde/ vnto the moost studyous and vertuous yonge mayde Fraunces S. sendeth gretynge and well to fare.

I haure herde many men put great dout/whether it shulde be expedyent and requisite or nat/ a woman to haue lernyng in bokes of latyn and greke. And some vtterly affyrme that it is nat onely/ nother necessarye nor profytable/ but also very noysome and ieoperdous: Allegyng for their opinion that the frayle kynde of women/ beyng enclyned of their owne corage vnto vice/ and muta-ble at euery newelty/ if they shulde haue skyll in many thinges/ that

be written in the latyn and greke tong/ compiled and made with
great crafte and eloquence/ where the mater is happely somtyme
more swete vnto the eare/ than holsome for the mynde/ it wolde
of lykelyhode/ bothe enflame their stomakes a great deale the
more/ to that vice/ that men saye they be to moche gyuen vnto of
their owne nature alredy/ and enstructe them also with more
subtilyte and conueyaunce/ to sette forwarde and accomplysshe
their frowarde entente and purpose. But these men that so say/
do in my iugement/ eyther regarde but lyttel what they speke in
this mater/ or els/ as they be for the more parte vnlerned/ they
enuy it/ and take it sore to hert/ that other shulde haue that
precious iewell/ whiche they nother haue theymselfe/ nor can
fynde in their hertes to take the payne to gette. For fyrste/ where
they reken suche instabilite and mutable nature in women/ they
saye therin their pleasure of a contensyous mynde/ for the mayn-
tenaunce of their mater/ for if they wolde loke thereon with one
euyn eye/ and consydre the mater equally/ they shulde fynde and
well perceyue/ that women be nat onely of no lesse constancy and
discrecion than men/ but also more stedfast and sure to truste
vnto/ than they.

For whether I praye you was more light and more to be
discommended/ Helen that with moche labour and sute/ and
many craftye meanes/ was at the last ouercome and inticed
to go away with the kynges sonne of Troye: Or Parys/
whiche with ones syght of her/ was so doted in her loue/ that
neyther the great chere and kyndenesse shewed vnto hym of her
husbande kyng Menelaus/ nor shame of the abomynable dede/
nor feare of the peryll that was lyke to come thervpon/ nor the
drede of god/ myght let hym to conuey her awaye/ contrary to
all gentylnesse/ contrary to all ryght/ all lawes and conscience.
Nor the woman casteth her mynde neyther to one nor other of her
owne proper wyll/ whiche thyng is a sure token of an vpryght and
a stedfaste mynde/ but by the sute and meanes of the man: Whan
he with one loke of her/ is rauisshed of all his wyttes. Nowe if
here parauenture a man wolde saye/ yes/ they be moued as well
as men/ but they dissemble/ forbeare/ and wyll nat vtter theyr
stomakes/ nother it is so conuenyent the woman to speke as the
man: that shall nat helpe his excuse/ but rather hyndre it/ for
they be the more worthy to be allowed/ that wyll nat be so farre
ouersene in that affection/ which is so naturally gyuen to all
thynges lyuyng/ but that they can remembre theyr duetie and

honestie/ where the man is many tymes so farre beside his reason/
that he seeth nother where nor whan/ nother to whom/nor howe
to behaue hymselfe/ nother can regarde/ what is comely and what
is nat. For verily/ it is as vnconuenient for the man to demaunde
that thynge that is vnlaufull/ if he coude perceyue/ as for the
woman. And if bothe theyr vyces were all open and shewed/ the
man shulde haue moche more that he ought to be ashamed of/
sauyng that he is also in that poynt worse than the woman/ in as
moche as she is ashamed of her faute/ be it neuer so small: and
he is so farre from that vertue/ that whan he hath done nought/
he reioyseth of it and auaunceth hymselfe/ as though it were well
done. And yet he is so vnreasonable in iugyng the woman/ that
as Isocrates saythe wherin he hathe no consyderation/ howe ofte
or howe sore he offende his wyfe: He wyll nat suffre ones to be
offended hymselfe by her neuer so lytell: where he wolde that she
shulde take his dedes all well in worthe. Wherfore indede/ women
be in gaye case and happy/ if their honestie and prayse must hange
at the gyrdelles of such people. Nowe as for lernyng/ if it were
cause of any yuell as they say it is/ it were worse in the man than
in the woman/ bicause (as I haue said here before) he can bothe
worse staye and refrayne hymselfe/ than she. And moreouer than
that/ he cometh ofter and in mo occasyons thanne the woman/
inasmoche/ as he lyueth more forthe abrode amonge company
dayly/ where he shal be moued to vtter suche crafte as he hath
gotten by his lernynge. And women abyde moost at home/ occupied euer with some good or necessary busynesse. And the latyn
and the greke tonge/ I se nat but there is as lytell hurt in them/
as in bokes of Englisshe and frenche/ whiche men bothe rede
themselfe/ for the proper pastymes that be written in them/ and
for the witty and craftie conueyaunce of the makynges: And also
can beare well ynoughe/ that women rede them if they wyll/
neuer so moche/ whiche commoditeis be farre better handeled in
the latyn and greke/ than any other langage: and in them be many
holy doctours writinges/ so deuout and effectuous/ that whosoeuer
redeth them/ muste nedes be eyther moche better or lesse yuell/
whiche euery good body bothe man and woman wyll rede and
folowe/ rather than other. But as for that/ that I here many men
ley for the greattest ieopardy in this mater/ in good faythe to be
playne me thynke it is so folysshe/ that scantly it is worthy/
eyther to be rehersed or answered vnto. That is/ where they saye/

if their wyues coulde Latyn or greke/ than myght they talke more
boldely with preesetes and freres/ as who sayth/ there were no
better meanes (if they were yll dysposed) to execute their pur-
poses/ than by spekynge Latyn or greke/outher els/ that preestes
and freres were commenly so well lerned/ that they can make
their bargeyne in latyn and greke so redily/ whiche thing is also
farre contrary/ that I suppose noweadayes a man coude nat deuyse
a better waye to kepe his wyfe safe from them/ than if he teche
her the latyn and greke tonge/ and suche good sciences as are
written in them: the whiche nowe most parte of preestes/ and
specially suche as be nought/ abhorre and flye from: ye/ as faste
in a maner/ as they flye from beggars that aske them almesse
in the strete. And where they fynde faute with lernyng/ bycause
they say/ it engendreth wytte and crafte/ there they reprehende it/
for that that it is moost worthy to be commended for/ and the
whiche is one singuler cause wherfore lernyng ought to be desyred/
for he that had leuer haue his wyfe a foole than a wyse woman/
I holde hym worse than twyse frantyke. Also/ redyng and study-
eng of bokes so occupieth the mynde/ that it can haue no leyser
to muse or delyte in other fantasies/ whan in all handywerkes/
that men saye be more mete for a woman/ the body may be busy
in one place/ and the mynde walkyng in another: and while they
syt sowing and spinning with their fyngers/ maye caste and com-
passe many peuysshe fantasyes in their myndes/ whiche must
nedes be occupyed/ outher with good or badde/ so long as they
be wakynge. And those that be yuell disposed/ wyll fynde the
meanes to be nought/though they can neuer a letter on the booke/
and she that wyll be good/lernyng/ shall cause her to be moche
the better. For it sheweth the ymage and wayes of good lyuynge/
euyn right as a myrrour sheweth the symylitude and proporcion of
the body. And doutlesse/ the daylye experyence prouethe/ that
suche as are nought/ are those than neuer knewe what lernyng
ment. For I neuer herde tell/ nor reed of any woman well lerned/
that euer was (as plentuous as yuell tonges be) spotted or inflamed
as vicious. But on the other side/ many by their lernyng taken
suche encreace of goodnesse/ that many may beare them wyt-
nesse of their vertue/ of whiche sorte I coulde reherse a great
nombre/ bothe of olde tyme and late/ Sauynge that I wyll be con-
tente as for nowe/ with one example of oure owne countre and
tyme/ that is: this gentylwoman/ whiche translated this lytell

boke herafter folowyng: whose vertuous conuersacion/ lyuyng/ and sadde demeanoure/ maye be profe euydente ynough/ what good lernynge dothe/ where it is surely roted: of whom other women may take example of prudent/ humble/ and wyfely be-hauour/ charitable and very christen vertue/ with whiche she hath with goddes helpe endeuoured herselfe/ no lesse to garnisshe her soule/ than it hath lyked his goodnesse with lovely beauty and comelynesse/ to garnysshe and sette out her body: And undouted is it/ that to th yncrease of her vertue/ she hath taken and taketh no lytell occasyon of her lernyng/ besydes her other manyfolde and great commodyteis taken of the same/ amonge whiche commodyteis this is nat the leest/ that with her vertuous/ worshipfull/ wyse/ and well lerned husbande/ she hath by the occasyon of her lernynge/ and his delyte therin/ suche especiall conforte/ pleasure/ and pastyme/ as were nat well possyble for one vnlerned couple/ eyther to take togyder or to conceyue in their myndes/ what pleasure is therin. Therfore good Fraunces/ seyng that suche frute/ profite and pleasure cometh of lernyng/ take uo hede vnto the leude wordes of those that dispreyse it/ as verily no man dothe/ saue suche as neyther haue lernyng/ nor wotteth what it meaneth/ which is indede the moost parte of men/ and as the moost parte and the best parte be nat alwaye of one mynde/ so if this mater shulde be tryed/ nat by wytte and reason/ but by heedes or handes/ the greater parte is lyke as it often dothe/ to vanquisshe and ouercome the better/ for the best parte (as I reken)/ whom I accompte the wysest of euery age/ as among the Gentyls the olde philosophers/ and among the christen men/ the auncient doctors of Christes churche/ all affyrme lernyng to be very good and profitable/ nat onely for men but also for women/ the whiche Plato the wyse philosopher calleth a bridell for yonge people agaynst vice. Wherfore good Fraunces/ take you the best parte and leaue the moost/ folowe the wyse men and regarde nat the folysshe sorte/ but applye all your myght/ wyll/ and dilygence to optayne that especiall treasure/ whiche is delectable in youthe/ comfortable in age/ and profytable at all seasons: Of whom with-out doute/ cometh moche goodnesse and vertue. Whiche vertue whoso lacketh/ he is without that thing that onely maketh a man: Ye and without the whiche a man is worse than an vnreasonable beest/ nor ones worthy to haue the name of a man. It maketh fayre and amyable/ that that is of nature deformed: as Diogynes

the philosopher/ whan he sawe a yong man foule and yuell
fauoured of persone/ but very vertuous of lyuenge: thy vertue
sayd he/ maketh the beautifull: And that that is goodly of itselfe
alredy/ it maketh more excellent and bright. Whiche as Plato the
wyse philosopher saythe/ if it coude be sene with our bodily eyes/
it wolde make men wondersly enamored and taken in the loue of
it. Wherfore vnto those especiall giftes of grace that god hath
lent you/ and endewed you with all/ endeuer youreselfe that this
precyous diamonde and ornament be nat lackyng/ whiche had/
shall florishe and lyghten all your other giftes of grace/ and make
them more gaye: and lacked/ shall darke and blemysshe them
sore. And surely the beautie of it/ though ye had none other/
shall gette you bothe greatter loue/ more faithfull and lengar to
contynue of all good folkes/ than shall the beautie of the body/
be it neuer so excellent/ whose loue decayeth togyder/ with it
that was the cause of it/ and moost commenly before/ as by dayly
experyence we maye se/ them that go toguyder for the loue of
the bodily beautie/ within a small whyle whan their appetyte is
satisfyed/ repent themselfe. But the loue that cometh by the
meanes of vertue and goodnesse shall euer be fresshe and en-
crease/ ryght as dothe the vertue itselfe. And it shall you come
by none otherwise so redily/ as if you contynue the study of
lernyng/ whiche you be entred well in allredy: And for your tyme
and age/ I wolde saye/ had greatly profyted/ sauynge that chyldes
age is is so frayle accompted/ that it nedeth rather monicion and
contynuall callynge vpon/ than the deserued prayse: Howe be it
I haue no doute in you/ whome I se naturally borne vnto vertue/
and hauyng so good bringyng vp of a babe/ nat onely among your
honourable vncles chyldren/ of whose conuresacion and company/
they that were right yuell/ might take occasyon of goodnesse and
amendement/ But also with your owne mother/ of whose preceptes and teachyng/ and also very vertuous lyueng/ if you take
hede/ as I put no feare you wyll and also do/ you cannot fayle
to come to suche grace and goodnesse/ as I haue euer had opynion
in you that ye shulde. Wherfore I haue euer in my mynde fauored
you/ and forthered to my power your profite/ and encrease
thervnto/ and shall as long as I se you delyte in lernynge and
vertue/ no kynde of payne or labour refused on my partie/ that
maye do you good. And as a token of my good mynde/ and
an instrument towarde our successe and furtheraunce I sende you

this boke/ lytell in quantite but bigge in value/ tourned out of
latyn into englysshe by your owne forenamed kynswoman/
whose goodnesse and vertue/ two thynges there be that let me
moche to speke of. The one/ bicause it were a thyng superfluous
to spende many words vnto you about that mater/ which your-
selfe knowe well ynough/ by long experience and dayly vse. The
other cause is/ for I wolde eschewe the sclaundre of flatery:
howe be it I count it no flatery to speke good of them that
deserue it/ but yet I knowe that she is as lothe to haue prayse
gyuyn her/ as she is worthy to haue it/ and had leauer her prayse
to reste in mennes hertes/ than in their tonges/ or rather in
goodes estimacion and pleasure/ than any mannes wordes or
thought: and as touchynge the boke itselfe/ I referre and leaue
it to the iugementes of those that shall rede it/ and vnto suche
as are lerned/ the onely name of the maker putteth out of
question/ the goodnesse and perfectyon of the worke/ which as
to myne owne opinyon and fantasye/ can nat be amended in any
poynte: And as for the translacion therof/ I dare be bolde to say
it/ that whoso lyst and well can conferre and examyne the trans-
lacyon with the originall/ he shall nat fayle to fynde that she hath
shewed herselfe/ nat onely erudite and elegant in eyther tong/
But hath also vsed suche wysedom/ suche dyscrete and substan-
cyall iudgement in expressynge lyuely the latyn/ as a man maye
parauenture mysse in many thynges/ translated and tourned by
them that bare the name of right wise and very well lerned men:
and laboure that I haue had with it about the printing/ I yelde
holly and frely gyue vnto you/ in whose good maners and vertue/
as in a chylde/ I haue so great affection/ and vnto your good
mother/ vnto whom I am so moche beholden/ of whose company
I take so great ioye and pleasure/ in whose godly communycacion
I fynde such spyrituall frute and swetnesse/ that as ofte as I talke
with her/ so ofte me thynke I fele myselfe the better. Therfore
nowe good Fraunces folowe styll on her steppes/ looke euer vpon
her lyfe/ to enfourme your owne therafter/ lyke as ye wolde
loke in a glasse to tyre your body by : ye/ and that more dili-
gentlye/ insomoche as the beautie of the body though it be neuer
so well attended/ wyll soone fade and fall awaye: good lyuyng
and vertue ones gotten tarieth styll/ whose frute ye shall fele/
nat onely in this worlde whiche is transytorie and of shorte con-
tynuance/ but also in another: And also it shulde be great shame/

dishonestye/ and rebuke vnto you borne of suche a mother/ and also nourysshed vp with her owne teate/ for to degenerate and go out of kynde. Beholde her in this age of hers/ in this almost contynuall disease and syckenesse/ howe busye she is to lerne/ and in the small tyme that she hath had/ howe moche she hath yet profited in the latin tonge/ howe great comforte she taketh of that lernynge that she hath gotten/ and consydre therby what pleasure and profite you maye haue hereafter (if god lende you lyfe (as I praye he do) of the lernyng that you may haue or you come to her age/ if you spende your tyme well: whiche doyng you shall be able to do youreselfe good/ and be great ioye and comforte to all your frendes/ and all that euer wolde you well/ among whom I wolde you shulde reken me for one/ nat amonge the leest yf nat amonge the chefe: and so fare you well/ myne owne good/ gentyll/ and fayre Fraunces. At Chelcheth/ the yere of our lorde god/ a thousande fyue hundred xxiiij. The first day of Octobre.

*　　*　　*

Hereafter folowethe seuyn peticions of the Pater noster/ translated out of Latyn into Englysshe.

The fyrst peticion.

Pater noster qui es in celis/ sanctificetur nomen tuum. Here O father in heuyn the petycions of thy chyldren/ whiche thoughe they be as yet bodily in erthe/ nat withstandynge/ in mynde euer they desyre and long to come to the countre celestiall/ and fathers house/ where they well knowe and vnderstande/ that the treasure of euerlastyng welthe and felycite/ that is to saye/ the inherytaunce of lyfe immortall/ is ordayned for theym. We aknowledge thyne excellency/ O maker/ sauyour/ and gouernour of all thyng/ conteyned in heuen and in erthe/ And agayne we aknowledge and confesse our owne vylesnesse/ and in nowyse we durst be so bolde to call the father (whiche are farre vnworthy to be thy bondemen/ ne take vpon vs the most honorable name of thy children/ whiche vnneth thou vouchsauest thyne angelles/ except thy mere goodnesse hadde: by adoptyon receyued vs into the great honour of this name. The tyme was/ whan we were seruauntes to wyckednesse and synne/ by the miserable generacion of Adam: we were also children of the fende/ by whose instinction and spyrite we were driuen and compelled to euery kynde of myschefe and

offence. But that thou of thyne infinite mercy/ by thyne onely be-
goten sonne Jesus/ made vs free from the thraldome of synne/
and delyueredest vs from the deuyll our father/ and by violence
riddest vs from th inheritaunce of eternall fyre/ and at the last/
thou vouchsaffest to adopt vs by faythe and baptyme/ as membres
in the moost holy body of thy sonne: nat onely into the felowshyppe
of thy name/ but also of thyne inheritaunce. And bycause we
shulde nothyng mystrust in thy loue towarde vs/ as a sure token
therof/ thou sendest from heuen downe into oure hertes/ the
moost holy spyrite of thy sonne: whiche (all seruauntlye feares
shaken of) boldely cryeth out in our hertes without cessyng/
Abba pater/ whiche in Englysshe is as moche to saye/ as O
father father: and this thy sonne taught vs/ by whome (as
mynister) thou gyuest vs all thynge: That whan we were as it
were borne agayne by thy spyrite/ and at the fontstone in bap-
tyme/ renounced and forsaken our father the deuyll/ and had
begon to haue no father in erthe/ than we shulde aknowledge
onely oure father celestyall: By whose marueylous power we were
made somwhat of ryght nought: by whose goodnesse we were
restored/ whan we were loste: by whose wysedome incomparable/
euermore we are gouerned and kepte/ that we fall nat agayne into
distruction. This thy sonne gaue vs full truste to call vpon the/
he assigned vs also a way of prayeng to the/ aknowledge therfore
the desire and prayer of thy sonne/ aknowledge the spirite of thy
sonne/ whiche prayeth to thy maiestie for vs by vs: Do thou nat
disdayne to be called father of those/ whom thy sonne moost
lykest thy ymage/ vouchesafe to call his brethern/ and yet we
ought nat hervpon to take lykyng in ourselves/ but to gyue glorie
to the and thy sonne for that great gentylnesse: sithe no man can
here of hymselfe ought deserue/ but that thyng whatsoeuer good
it be/ cometh of thy onely and free lyberalite. Thou delytest
rather in names louyng and charitable/ than terrible and fearefull:
Thou desyrst rather to be called a father/ thanne a lorde or
maister: Thou woldest we shulde rather loue the as thy children/
than feare the as thy seruauntes and bondemen: Thou fyrst
louedest vs/ and of thy goodnesse also it cometh/ and thy
rewarde/ that we do loue the agayne. Gyue eare/ O father of
spyrites to thy chyldren spyrituall/ whiche in spyrite praye to the:
For thy sonne tolde vs/ that in those that so prayed thy delyte
was/ whom therfore thou sendest into the worlde that he shulde

teache vs all veryte and trouthe. Here nowe the desyres of vnyte
and concorde/ for it is nat sytting ne agreable/ that bretherne
whom thy goodnesse hath put in equall honoure/ shulde disagre
or varry among themselfe/ by ambicious desyre of worldely
promocion/ by contencious debate/ hatered or enuy/ all we hang
of one father/ we all one thyng praye for and desyre/ no man
asketh ought for hymselfe specially or a parte/ but as membres
of one body/ quyckened and releued with one soule: we requyre
and praye in commen/ for that whiche indyfferently shal be
expedient and necessary for vs all. And indede/ we dare none
other thyng desyre of the/ than what thy sonne commaunded
vs/ ne otherwise aske/ than as he apoynted vs/ for in so askyng/
his goodnesse promysed we shulde optayne/ whatsoeuer we
prayed for in his name. And for as moche as whan thy sonne
was here in erthe/ he nothyng more feruently desyred/ than that
thy moost holy name shulde appere and shyne/ nat onely in
Judea/ but also thorowe all the worlde/ besyde we also/ bothe
by his encoragyng and ensample/ this one thing aboue all desyre/
that the glorie of thy most holy name/ maye replenisshe and
fulfyll bothe heuen and erthe/ so that no creature be whiche
dredeth nat thy hye power and maieste/ whiche do nat worshippe
and reuerende also thy wysdome eternall and marueylous good-
nesse/ for thy glorie as it is great/ so neyther hauyng begynnyng
nor endyng/ but euer in itselfe florisshynge/ can neyther encreace
nor decreace/ but it skylleth yet mankynde nat a lytell/ that euery
man it knowe and magnifye/ for to knowe and confesse the onely
very god. And Jesus Christ whom thou sendest into the worlde is
as moche to vs/ as lyfe eternall. Let the clere shynyng of thy
name/ shadowe and quenche in vs all worldly glory. Suffre no
man to presume to take vpon hymselfe any parte of glory/ for
glory out of the is non/ but very sclaundre and rebuke. The
course of nature also in carnall children this thyng causeth/ that
they greatlye desyre the good fame and honest reputacion of
their father: for we maye se howe glad they be/ and howe they
reioyce/ howe happy also they thynke themselfe/ if happen their
fathers and great honoure/ as goodly tryumphe/ or their ymage
and picture to be brought into the court or commen place with an
honourable preface/ or any other goodly royalte whatsoeuer it
be. And agayne we se how they wayle/ and howe agast and
astonyed they be/ if chaunce their fathers sclaundre or infamy.

So depely hath this thyng naturall affection routed in mannes hert/ that the fathers reioyse in their childrens glory/ and their children in the glorie of their fathers. But for as moche as the gostly loue and affection of god/ farre passeth and excedeth the carnall affection of man: therfore we thy spirituall children/ moche more feruently thurst and desyre the glory and honour of thy most holy name/ and greatly are vexed and troubled in hert/ if he/ to whom alone all glorye is due chaunce rebuked or sclaundred to be/ nat that any sclaundre or rebuk can mynisshe or defoule the clerenesse of thy glory/ but that we/ as moche as lyeth in vs/ in a maner do wronge and iniury to thy name/ whansoeuer the gentyls eyther nat knowyng/ or elles dispisynge the maker and originall of all/ do worshippe and homage to creatures most vyle/ as made of tymbre or stone: or other peynted images/ some also to orensome to bulles/ and suche other lyke: And moreouer/ in all these foule and wycked deuylles/ in honour of them they sing hymnes: to these they do sacrifyce/ before these they burne ensence and other swete sauorurs/ than we thy spirytuall chyldren seyng all this/ doubly are agreued/ bothe that thou hast nat that honour whiche is due to the/ and that these wretches perisshe by their owne madnesse and follye. The iewes also neuer cesse in their sinagoges and resorte of people/ from dispitefull and abominable bacbytinge of thy onely sonne/ wherby in the meanetyme they sclaundre the/ sithe it can nat be chosen whan thy sonne is misfamed (whiche is the very clerenesse of thy glorie) but that infamy also must redounde in the. They cast eke in our tethe/ as a thyng of great dishonestie/ the most glorious name of thy chyldren/ sayeng/ that it were better to be called theues or manquellers/ thanne christen men and folowers of Christ. They ley agaynst vs also that thy sonne was crucified/ whiche is to vs great glorie and renoume/ we maye thanke thy mercy, father of all this thyng that we haue/ and aknowledge the as originall and causer of all oure helthe/ that we worshyppe also thy sonne in egall authorite with the/ and that we haue receyued into our hertes the spirite of you bothe. But yet good father in heuen/ we pray the to shewe thy mercy to those also/ that bothe the gentyls leauyng and forsakyng the worshippyng and homage of counterfaite ymages: maye do all honour and reuerence to thy maiestie alone/ and the iewes releued with thy spyrite/ renounsing their supersticious vsyng of the lawe maye confesse god/ from whom all thyng so

abundantly cometh/ may confesse the sonne of god/ by whome
we receyue all: maye confesse the holy gost/ parttaker and felowe
of the diuyne nature/ Let them worshippe in thre persons/ one
and egall maiestie/ and aknowledge thre persons as one proper
persone/ so that euery nacyon/ euery tonge/ euery secte/ euery
age/ as well olde as yong/ maye with one assent auaunce and
praise thy moost holy name. And I wolde to god that we also/
whiche beare the name of thy children/ were nat dishonestie to
thy glorie/ amongest those that knowe the nat: for lyke as a
good and wise sonne is the glorie and honour of his father/ so
a folisshe and vnthrifty childe/ getteth his father dishonestie and
shame/ and he is nat a naturall and proper chylde/ whosoeuer
do nat labour all that he can to folowe and be like his father in
wytte and condicions: But thy sonne Jesus is a very kynde and
naturall childe/ for he is a very full and perfite ymage and
similitude of the/ whom holly he is lyke and representeth. We
whiche are become thy children by adopcion and nat by nature/
confermyng ourselves after his ensample/ endeauer as moche as
lyeth in vs/ to come to some maner lykenesse of the: that lykewise as thou waste moost parfitely exalted and glorified in thy
sonne Jesus: so as far forth as our weakenesse wyll suffre/ thou
mayst be glorified also in vs/ but the wayes howe thou mayst be
glorified in vs/ is/ if the worlde perceyue that we lyue after the
teaching and doctrine of thy sonne that is to say/ if they se that
we loue the aboue all thyng/ and our neighbour and brother no
lesse than our owne selues/ and that we euer beare good mynde
and loue to our ennemy and aduersary/ also well doing and
profyting those/ whiche do vs injury and wrong: for these thynges
thy sonne badde vs we shulde do/ whan he prouoked vs to the
folowyng and likenesse of our father in heuen/ whiche com-
maundeth his sonne to shyne vpon good and yuell: And howe
great a shame and dyshoneste are they to thy glorie/ whiche whan
they haue professed and taken vpon them thy name/ natwith-
standynge/ do robbery and thefte: commyt aduoutrie: chyde and
braule: study to reuenge: go about to disceyue: forswere theym-
selfe by thy moost holy name: amonge also sclaundre and backe-
byte: haue their belly as their god: dispyce the/ and do seruice
and homage to worldely richesse. And truely the commen sorte
of people for the moost parte/ esteme god after the lyueng and
condicions of his seruauntes. For if they may parceyue that they

whiche haue professed thy name/ lyue viciouslye: thanne they
crye out and saye. What a god is he that hath suche maner of
worshippers. Fye on suche a mayster that hath so vnrewly
seruauntes: Out vpon such a father/ whose children be so leude:
Banished be suche a kyng/ that hath suche maner of people and
subiectes. Thy sonne therfore consydring this/ taught vs that
lykewise as he bothe lyueeng and dyeng euer glorified thy name
so we also all that we might/ shulde endeuer by chast and blame-
lesse condicions/ to auaunce and preyse the clerenesse of thy
glorie/ sayeng vnto vs. Let your light shine in the sight of men/
that they maye se your good workes/ and in those glorify your
father in heuen. But in vs O good father/ there is no lyght at all/
excepte it wyll please the to sende vs any/ whiche arte the contynuall and euerlastyng spring of all lyght: nor we of ourselves can
bring forthe no good workes. Therfore good lorde we praye the/
lette thy goodnesse worke in vs/ and thy clere lyght shine in vs: as
in all thynge that thou hast created/ dothe shine they eternall and
endlesse power/ thy wysdome vnable to be expressed and thy
wonderfull goodnesse whiche moost specially/ yet thou vouch-
safest to shewe to mankynde. Nowe than whydersoeuer we loke/
all thynges glorifye thy name: the erthely spirites bothe day and
nyght neuer lynne prayeng their lorde and kyng: the wonderfull also
and heuenly ingen that we beholde: the disagreyng concorde
moreouer of the clamentes: the flowing and ebbyng of the see:
the bublisshyng of ryuers: the enduring courses of waters: so many
dyuers kyndes of thynges/ so many kyndes of trees and of herbes/
so many of creatures/ and to euerythyng the proper apoynted
and sette nature: As in the Adamant stone to drawe yron/ the
herbes to cure and heale diseases and sickenesse: All these
thynges I saye/ what other thyng do they shewe to vs than the
glorie of thy name/ and that thou arte onely very god/ onely
immortall/ onely of all power and might/ onely wyse/ onely
good/ onely mercyfull/ onely Juste/ onely trewe/ onely maruey-
lous/ onely to be loued and had in reuerence. Than father/ we
may well se that he doth wrong to thy glorious name/ whosoeuer
take vpon himself to be called by any of these names/ for though
there be in vs any of these rehersed vertues/ yet all that cometh
to vs from thy liberall goodnesse. Graunt nowe therfore father/
that thy name on euery side be glorified/ and that the light and
glory of thy name/ maye no lesse appere and shyne in our maners

and lyuenge/ than it shyneth in thy Angels/ and in all thynge that thou hast created and made: that in lykewise as they/ whiche beholde and loke vpon this worlde of the wonderfull and marueylous workemanshippe/ do guesse the excellency of the maker therof: so they that knowe the nat: moued and stered by our example/ maye bothe confesse their owne misery and wretchednes and marueile thy liberall goodnesse/ and by these meanes turned and conuerted/ may togyder with vs glorify the most holy name of the/ of thy sonne/ and of the holy gost/ to whom indifferently all honour and glorie is due foreuer. Amen.

The seconde peticion.

A *dueniat regnum tuum.* O father in heuen/ whiche arte the onely causer/ maker/ sauiour/ restorer/ and gouernour of all/ bothe in heuen and in erthe/ out of whom cometh and procedeth all authorite/ power/ kyngdome/ and rule/ as well to thynges vncreated as created/ as well to thinges inuisible as visible/ whose trone and seate of maiestie is the heuen: and the erthe as fotestole: whose kyngly septre and mace/ is thyne eternall and most establisshed wyll/ whom no power is able to withstande. Ones thou promisest thy people by the mouthes of thy prophetes/ for the helth of mankynde/ a certayne spirituall realme/ whiche shulde bryng into liberte/ those that were thyne and borne anewe in the/ and shulde delyuer them out of the tyrannous handelyng of the fende/ whiche in tyme past raigned as prince in the worlde/ sore entangled and combred with synne. And to the gettyng and optaynynge of this realme/ thou vouchsauest to sende from heuen downe into the erthe thy onely sonne/ whiche with the losse of his owne lyfe/ redemynge vs/ where we were afore seruauntes of the deuyll/ shulde make vs the children of god: and verily thy sonne/ while he lyued here in erthe/ was wont to call his gospell/ the heuenly kyngdome and the realme of god: whose knowlege yet he sayde/ to be hydde and kepte secrete from vs/ but nat withstandyng/ thy children humbly require/ and with feruente desyre/ beseke the that this realme/ whiche our lorde Jesus chalenged for the/ myght daylye more and more be disclosed and opyned here in erth/ vntyll that tyme come/ in whiche that same thy sonne shall restore and rendre it vp to the full and hole/ whan all those haue subdued themselfe/ whom thy goodnesse or the begynnyng of the worlde hath apoynted to dwell in this realme. And whan all obstinate and rebelleous spirites/ and all malycious and yuell desyres be fully quenched and wyped away/ whiche hiderto and at this day/ make warre and insurrection agaynst thy maieste/ whiche vexe and vnquiete thy communalte/ what time thy royalme shal be in sure peace and tranquillite: For verily as yet the worlde/ by all the meanes and subtilties it can/ oppresseth thy children/ wandryng here bodily in erth as yet: also corrupt and vnclene affections/ and olde originall synne/ rebell and striue ayenst the spirite: as yet noyous and wycked spirites/ whiche thou banyssheddest/ and put out of the heuenly cite/ do assaut with fyrely dartes from aboue those/ whom thou of thy mere goodnesse hast deuyded from this worlde/ and as chosen folke and parttakers of thy sonne/ hast apoynted to thy royalme. Graunt father of all myght/ that they/ whom thy goodnesse ones hath delyuered from the tyranny of synne/ and assygned to dwell in thy royalme/ maye by the benifitte of the same benygne goodnesse contynue/ and stedfastly abyde in theyr liberte and fredome: and that none leauynge and fayling from the and thy sonne/ retourne agayne in the tyrannous seruice of the deuyll : and so bothe by thy sonne shall raigne in the to our welthe/ and thou in vs to thy glorie: for thou art glorified in our blysse/ and our blysse is of thy goodnesse. Thy sonne Jesus taught vs we shulde dispice the realme of this worlde/ whiche standeth all by rychesse/ and is holde vp by garrisons of men/ by hostes and armour/ which also whatsoeuer it doth/ dothe by pryde and violence/ and is both gotten/ kept/ and defended by fierse cruelnesse: and he with the holy goost/ ouercame the wycked spirite that ruled as chefe and heed in the worlde: afore he by innocency and purenesse of lyuyng/ had the victorie of synne/ by mekenesse venquesshed cruelnesse/ by suffraunce of many dispitefull rebukes/ recouered euerlastyng glory/ by his owne deth restored life/ and by his crosse had triumphe vpon the wycked spirites. Thus wonderfully hast thou father warred and ouercome: after this maner thou both triumphest and reignest in thy sonne Jesus/ by whom it hath pleased the of thy goodnesse/ to take vs into the congregacion of the dwellers in thy royalme. Thus also thou tryumphest and reignest in thy holy martyrs/ in thy chast virgins and pure confessours/ whiche yet neyther by theyr owne strength nor power/ dyde ouercome the fiersenesse and displeasure of tyrantes/ ne the raging or the wantonnesse of the flesshe/ ne the maliciousnesse of this worlde. But it was thy

spirite father/ which it pleased the to gyue them to the glorie
of thy name/ and the helthe of mankynde/ that was bothe the
begynner and ender of all this in them: And we rather/ hertely
desire the/ that thy realme may florisshe also in vs: whiche allthough we do no myracles/ for as moche as neyther tyme nor
mater requireth: albeit we be nat imprysoned nor turmented:
though we be nat wounded nor brent/ although we be nat crucified
nor drowned: thoughe we be nat beheeded: yet nat withstandyng/
the strength and clerenesse of thy realme: may shine and be noble
in vs/ if the worlde perceyue/ that we by the helpe of thy spirite/
stande stedfast and sure agaynst all assautes of the deuyll/ and
agaynst the flesshe: whiche alwaye stereth and prouoketh vs to
those thynges/ that be contrary to the spirite/ and agaynst the
worlde/ whiche by all the wayes it can/ moueth vs to forsake
and leaue the trust that we haue ones put in the/ As often soeuer
as for thy loue we despice and sette nought by the realme of this
worlde/ and with full trust hange vpon the heuenly kyngdome/
that thou hast promysed vs: as often also/ as we forsake and
leaue honourynge of erthely richesse/ and onely worshyp and
embrace the precious and gostly lernyng of the gospel/ as often
as we refuse those thynges/ that for the season seme swete and
pleasaunt to the flesshely and carnal appetite/ and in hope and
trust of eternall felicite we suffre paciently and valiantly all thynge/
be it neuer so harde: as often also as we can be content to forsake our naturall affections/ and that whiche we haue moost dere
as our fathers and mothers/ wyues/ chyldren/ and kynsefolke/
for the loue of the: Likewise as often as we oppresse and refrayne
the furious and fiercely braydes of angre and gyue mylde and meke
wordes/ to those that chyde and oraule with vs/ and do good
to them/ which do vs iniury and wronge: and all for thy sake.
So often father thou warrest in vs/ and ouercomest the realme
of the deuyll/ and openyst the myght and power of thy realme.
Thus it hath pleased and lyked thy wysdome father/ by continuall
and greuous batayle/ to exercise/ confyrme/ and make stedfaste
the vertue and strengthe of thy people. Encrease suche strengthe
in thy children/ that they maye euer retourne stronger from their
batayle/ and that whan by lytell and lytell/ their enemies and
aduersaries myght is minysshed and broken thou mayest everyday more and more raygne in vs: But the tyme is nat yet come
good father/ in whiche all the worlde haue subdued themselfe to

thy yoke: For as yet/ that tyrannous fende hath ado with many and diuers nacions: There is nat yet one herde/ and one herdemayster/ whiche we hope shal be/ whan the iewes also shall bryng and submyt themselfe to the spirituall and gostely lernyng of the gospell: for yet many know nat howe great a liberte it is/ and what a dignite/ and how great a felicite/ to be subiectes to the heuenly realme: and that is the cause why they had rather be the seruauntes of the deuyll/ than thy children inheritours with Jesus/ and parttakers of the kyngdome of heuen/ and amongest those two father/ that walke within the cloyster of thy churche/ and seme as chefe in thy realme/ there are nat a fewe (alas) whiche holde on their aduersaries side: and as moche as lyeth in them/ abate/ shame/ and dishonest the glory of thy realme. Werfore we specially desyre and wisshe for that tyme/ whiche thou woldest none to knowe but thyselfe alone/ in whiche/ acordyng to the promyse of thy sonne/ thy angels shall come and make clene the floore of thy church/ and gader toguether into thy barne the pure corne/ deuyded and seuered fro the cockle/ and plucke out of thy realme/ all maner occasyon of sclaundre/ what tyme there shall neyther be hunger nor pouerte: no necessite of clothing: no disease: no dethe: no pursuer: no hurt or yuell at all/ ne any feare or suspicion of hurte/ but than all the body of thy dere sonne heaped togyder in theyr heed/ shall take fruicion and pleasure of thy blessed company of heuen. And they whiche in the meanetyme had rather serue the tyrannous fende/ shall togyther with their maister be banysshed and sente awaye to euerlastyng punisshement: And trewely this is the realme of Israel/ whiche whan Jesus Christ forsoke the erthe/ and retourned agayne to his disciples/ desyred/ myght shortely be restored. Than thou madest heuen free and rydde from all rebellion/ what tyme Lucifere with his company was caste out. So ones in the day of dome and iugement whan the bodyes shall aryse/ thou shalte departe the sheepe from the gottes: and than whosoeuer hath here with all diligence embrased the spirytuall and goostely realme of the gospell/ shal be desyred and brought to the/ to the inherytaunce of the euerlastynge kyngdome/ to the whiche thy goodnesse had apoynted theym or the worlde was made. This fortunate and happy day whiche thy sonne Jesus promysed shulde come/ we thy children good father/ greatlye desyre/ whiche dwelle here in erthe as outlawes in exyle/ sore lodened with the huge-

nesse of the erthely body/ suffryng in the meantyme/ many greuous
displeasures/ and sorowyng that we be withdrawen from thy com-
pany/ wherof than we shall haue perfite pleasure and fruycion/
Whan face to face we shall se and beholde our kyng and father/
raignyng in his great glorie. And yet we haue nat this hope and
truste of our owne merites and desertes/ whiche we knowe verily
as non/ but onely of thy liberall goodnesse: wherby it lyked the
to bestowe thyne owne sonne holly for vs/ and to sende vs the
holy goost as pledge and token of this inheritaunce: and if it wyll
please the also to graunt/ that we maye stedfastly and without any
waueryng/ contynue in thy sonne Jesus: than thou canst nat
departe vs from the company of thy realme: To whome with that
same thy sonne and the holy goost/ all renome/ honour/ and
glorie is due worlde without ende. Amen.

The thyrde peticion.

Fiat voluntas tua sicut in celo et in terra. O father whiche art
the noryssher and ordrer of all/ whom it pleaseth thy sonne to
aknowlege as his bretherne/ and he so aknowlegeth all those/ that
in pure faythe professeth his name in baptysme: Thy children here
in erthe call and crye to the dwellyng in heuen/ a place farre out
of all chaungeable mutabilite of thynges created/ desyryng indede/
to come to thy heuenly and celestiall company/ whiche is defouled
with no maner spotte of yuell/ sauyng they knowe well that non
can be taken and receyued into so great a tranquillite and quiet-
nesse/ but onely they/ whiche with busye studye/ whyle they
lyue here/ labour to be such as ther must be: Therfore it is all
one realme/ bothe of heuen and erthe/ sauyng this difference/
that here we haue sore and greuous confiicte with the flesshe/ the
worlde/ and the deuyll: and there allthough there is nothyng that
might minysshe or defoyle the welthe of blessed soules: Yet as
touchynge the full perfection of felicite/ there is some maner
mysse/ which is/ that all the membres and partes of thy sonne
be gathered together/ and that the hole body of thy sonne/ safe
and sounde be ioyned to his heed/ wherby neyther Christe shall
lacke any of his partes and membres/ nor good mennes soules
theyr bodyes: whiche lykewise as they were euer here in erthe
parttakers of theyr punisshementes and afflictions: so their desyre
is to haue them companions of their ioye in heuen. And they finally

in this worlde/ go about to folowe the vnite and concorde of the heuenly kyngedome/ whiche all the tyme they lyue bodily in erthe/ as it becometh naturall and obedient children/ studye with all diligence to fulfyll those thynges/ whiche they knowe shall content thy mynde and pleasure/ and nat what their owne sensuall appetite gyueth them/ ne iugyng or disputyng why thou woldest this or that to be done/ but thynkyng it sufficient/ that thus thou woldest it/ whom they knowe surely to wyll nothing/ but that that is best. And what thy will is/ we lerned sufficiently of thy onely begotten and moost dere sonne. He was obeydient to thy wyll/ euyn to his owne dethe/ and thus he sayd/ for our lernyng and instruction. Father/ if it may conuenyently be/ suffre this drynke of my passyon to be withdrawen from me/ howebeit/ yet thy wyll be fulfylled and nat myne. So that than nedes must man be ashamed/ to preferre and set forth his owne wyll/ if Christ our maister was content to cast his owne wyll awaye and subdue it to thyne. The flesshe hath his proper wyll and delyte/ whiche man naturally desyreth to kepe and folowe. The worlde also hath a wyll by itselfe/ and the deuyll his wyll/ farre contrarye to thyne. For the flesshe coueteth agaynst the spirite whiche we haue receyued of the: and the worlde entyseth vs to sette our loue on frayle and vanysshyng thynges: and the deuyll laboureth about that/ that might bring man to euerlasting distruction. Nor it is nat inough/ that in baptyme we haue professed/ that we wyll be obedient to thy preceptes/ and there to haue renounced the deuyls seruice/ excepte we labour all our lyfe/ to perfourme stedfastly that/ whiche we haue professed: But that we nat perfourme/ but if thou gyue vs strengthe/ to helpe forthe our purpose: so that our wyll haue no place in vs/ but let thy wyll father worke in vs that/ whiche thy wysdome iudgeth and thynketh best for vs. Whosoeuer lyueth after the flesshly and carnall appetite they are deed to the/ and than nat as thy children. Ye/ and we thy children also/ as longe as we are here bodily in erthe/ haue among nat a litell businesse and ado/ in venquesshyng the flesshly delite: whiche laboreth to preuent thy wyll: but graunt good father/ that thyne euer ouercome and haue the better/ whether it lyke the we lyue or dye/ or to be punisshed for our correction/ or be in prosperite/ to the entente we shulde gyue the thankes for thy liberall goodnesse. And they folowe and obeye the wyl of the deuyl/ whiche do sacrifice and homage to idols/ whiche sclaunderously backebite thy most honorable sonne/ and for enuy and yuell wyll/ go about to brynge theyr neyghbour into perill and distruction: and so they may shortly waxe ryche/ care nat whether they do ryght or wrong/ and are al fulfylled with corrupt and vnclene thoughtes/ But this is thy wyll father/ that we shulde kepe both our body and mynde chast and pure from al vnclenesse of the worlde/ and that we shulde preferre and set more by thyne honour and thy sonnes/ than all other thynges besyde. And that we shulde be angry with no man/ ne enuye or reuenge any man/ but alway be redy to do good for yuell: ye/ and to be content rather with turmentes/ hunger/ imprisonement/ banysshement/ and dethe/ than in any thynge to be contrarye to thy pleasure: And that we may be able euery day more and more/ to perfourme all this/ helpe vs O father in heuen/ that the flesshe may euer more and more be subiect to the spirite/ and our spirite of one assent/ and one mynde with thy spirite. And likewyse as nowe in dyuerse places thy children/ whiche are obedient to the gospell/ obey and do after thy wyll: so graunt they may do in all the worlde besyde/ that euery man may know and vnderstande/ that thou alone art the onely heed and ruler of althyng/ and that in lykewyse as there are none in heuen/ whiche mutter and rebell agaynst thy wyll/ so let euery man here in erthe/ with good mynde and gladde chere obey thy wyll and godly preceptes. Nor we can nat effectually and fully mynde what thou good lorde wyllest/ excepte it wyll please the to plucke and drawe vs therto. Thou commaundest vs to be obedyent to thy wyll and pleasure/ and indede they are nat worthy to be called children/ but if in all poyntes they folowe and obey theyr fathers byddyng: but sithe it hath liked thy goodnesse to take vs/ although farre vnworthy into so great an honour of thy name: let it please the also of thy gentylnesse to gyue vs a redy and stedfast wyll/ that in nothyng we ouerhippe or be agaynst that/ whiche thy godly and diuine wyll hath apoynted vs/ but that we kyll and mortifye our flesshly and carnall lustes/ and by thy spirite be ledde to the doyng of all good workes/ and althyng that is pleasaunt vnder thy sight. Wherby thou father mayst aknowledge vs as thy children naturall/ and nat out of kynde/ and thy sonne as kynde and good bretherne: that is to saye/ that bothe twayne maye aknowledge in vs his owne propre benefyte/ to whome with the holy goost equally and indifferent/ glorie is due foreuer. Amen.

The fourthe peticion.

Panem nostrum quotidianum da nobis hodie. O father in heuen/ whiche of thy excedyng goodnesse/ moost plentuously fedest all thynges that thou hast so wondersly created/ prouide for vs thy children/ whiche are chosen to dwelle in thy celestiall and heuenly house/ and that hang holly and onely of thy sonne/ some spirituall and goostly fode/ that we obeyng thy wyll and preceptes/ may dayly encrease and waxe bigger in vertue/ vntyl after the course of nature we haue optayned and gathered a full and perfyte strength in our lorde Jesus Christ. The children of this worlde/ so longe as they are nat banysshed ne out of theyr frendes fauour/ all that tyme they take lytell care of their meate and drynke: sithe their fathers of their tendre loue towarde them/ make sufficient prouision for them. Than moche lesse ought we to be carefull or studious/ whom thy sonne Jesus taught shulde caste away all care of the morowe meale/ perswadyng and assuring vs/ that so riche a father/ so gentyll/ so louynge/ and that had so great mynde of vs/ and whiche sente meat to the lytell byrdes/ and so nobly clotheth that lyles in the medowe/ wolde nat suffre his children/ whiche he hath endued with so honourable a name/ to lacke meate and bodily apparayle: but allthyng sette asyde that belongeth to the body/ we shulde specially and aboue all/ seke and labour about those thynges/ whiche pertayneth and belongeth to thy realme/ and the iustice therof. For as touching the iustes of the pharises that sauereth all carnally/ thou vtterly dispysest and settest nought by: For the spirituall iustes of thy realme/ standeth by pure faythe and vnfayned charyte. And it were no great mater or shewe of thy plentye/ to fede with breed made of corne the body/ whiche althoughe it perissshed nat for hunger/ yet it must nedes dye and perysshe within short space/ eyther by syckenesse/ age/ or other chaunce/ but we thy spirituall and goostly children/ desyre and craue of our spirituall father/ that spirituall and celestiall breed/ Wherby we are verily relyued/ whiche be verily and truely called thy children: that breed is thy worde full of all power/ bothe the gyuer and norissher of lyfe: Whiche breed thou vouchesauest to sende vs downe from heuen/ what tyme we were lyke to haue perissshed for hungre. For verily/ the breed and teachynge of the proude philosophers and pharises/ coude nat suffice and content our mynde: But that breed of thyne/ whiche

thou sendest vs/ restored deed men to lyfe/ of whiche whosoeuer
dothe eate shall neuer dye. This breed relyued vs: by this breed
we are norysshed and fatted: and by this we come vp to the perfite
and full strength of the spirite. This breed though day by day it
be eaten and distributed to euery vowell of the soule/ yet but if
thou father doest gyue it/ it is nat holsome nor anythyng auayleth.
The blessed body of thy dere sonne is the breed/ whereof we be
all parttakers/ that dwell within thy large house of the churche.
It is one breed that indifferently belongeth to vs all/ lykewyse
as we are but one body/ made of sondrye and diuers membres/
but yet quickened with one spirite: and though al take of this
breed/ yet to many it hath ben dethe and distruction/ for it can
nat be relefe/ but to suche as thou reachest it vnto/ mynglynge
it with thy heuenly grace/ by the reason wherof it maye be holsome
to the receyuours. Thy sonne is verite and trouth/ trouth also is
the breed and teachyng of the gospell/ whiche he lefte behynde
hym for our spirituall fode/ and this breed likewise to many hath
ben vnsauery/ which haue had the mouth of theyr soule out of
taste/ by the seuer of corrupte affections. But and it wyll please the
good father to gyue forthe this breed/ than it must of necessite
be swete and pleasaunt to the eaters: than it shal comfort those
that be in tribulation/ and plucke vp those that be slydden and
fallen downe/ and make stronge those that be sicke and weake/
and finally brynge vs to euerlasting lyfe. And for as moche as the
imbecilite and weakenesse of mannes nature/ is euer redy and apt
to declyne into the worse/ and the soule of man so contynually
assauted and layde at with so many subtile ingyns/ it is expedient
and necessary/ that thou dayly make stronge and hert thy children
with thy breed/ whiche elles are farre vnable to resyst so many
and so stronge ennemyes so many assautes/ and so many fearefull
and terrible dartes. For who father might abyde to be had in de-
rision of the worlde/ to be outlawed and banisshed/ to be putte
in prison: to be fettred and manacled: to be spoyled of all his
goodes/ and by stronge hande/ be depriued of the company of
his moost dere wyfe and wel beloued children/ but if nowe and
than/ he were hertened with thy heuenly and gostly breed. He
that teacheth the lernyng of the gospell/ he is he/ that gyueth vs
forthe this breed/ whiche yet he gyueth all in vayne/ except it be
also gyuen by the. Many there are/ whiche receyue the body
of thy sonne/ and that here the worde and doctryne of the gospell/

But they departe fro thence no stronger than they came/ bycause they haue nat deserued that thou good father/ shuldest priuely and inuisibly reache it forthe vnto them. This breed/ O most benigne father/ gyue thy children euery day/ vntyll that tyme come/ in whiche they shall eate of it/ at thy heuenly and celestiall table: wherby the children of thy realme shal be fulfylled with the plentuous abundancye of euerlastynge trouthe. And to take fruicion therof/ it were a marueylous felicite and pleasure/ whiche hath nede of none other thyng at all/ neyther in heuen nor erthe: For in the O father alone is all thynge/ out of whom is right nought to be desyred/ whiche toguyther with thy sonne and the holy gooste/ raygnest foreuer. Amen.

The fyfte peticion.

Et *dimitte nobis debita nostra/ sicut et nos dimittimus debitoribus nostris.* This is thy wyll and mynde O father in heuen/ whiche art the maker of peace and fauourer of concorde/ that thy chyldren/ whom it hath pleased thy goodnes to couple and ioyne in the bondes of one assent: and whom thou quickenest with one spirite/ and with one baptysme purgest and makest clene/ and in one house of the churche acompanyest/ and with the commen sacramentes of the churche doest norisshe: and whom thou hast indifferently called to the inheritaunce of the kyngedome of heuen/ bycause they shulde be of more strength/ and shulde lyue toguyder in thy house of one mynde: and that there shulde be no stryfe or contencion amongest the partes and membres of one body/ but eche to lyue in charite with other: Yet in so moche as they are fayne to kepe styll theyr mortall body/ it can nat be chose/ but by reason of the weakenesse and frailte of nature amonge/ displeasure and offences shall chaunce/ wherby though the clerenesse of brotherly loue and concorde be nat vtterly extinct and quenched/ yet it is made all faynt and colde/ and lyke in conclusion to be quenched: Except thou father of thy great gentylnesse and mercy/ shuldest dayly forgyue those that euery day offended the: for as often as we offende our brother/ so often also we offende and displease the father/ whiche commaundeddest we shulde loue our brother as our owne selfe/ but thy sonne knowyng well inough the imbecilite and weakenesse of this membre/ shewed vs a remedy therfore/ gyuyng vs sure hope that thy

goodnesse wolde remytte and forgyue vs all our offences/ if we on
the other side with all our hert wolde forgyue our brother/ whatsoeuer he trespaceth agaynste vs/ and this is a very equall and indifferent waye to optayne pardon and forgyuenesse/ which thy sonne
Jesus hath assigned: For howe can any man be so bolde to desyre
his father to withdrawe his reuengynnge hande from hym/ if he
hymselfe go about to reuenge a lytell offence in his brother/ or who
is of so shamelesse boldenesse/ that wolde nat be afrayde to saye
to the/ Slake thy angre/ whan he contynueth in rancoure and
malyce styll towarde his brother. And howe can he surely boost and
auaunce hymselfe as a membre of thy sonne/ whiche beyng fre
from all synne hymselfe/ prayde the to forgyue the theues on the
crosse/ if he all entangled with synne/ and a synner coulde nat
fynde in his hert to forgyue his brother/ agaynst whome nowe and
than he offendeth. So that amongest vs it maye be called rather
as mutuall chaunge of pardone/ than very forgyuenesse: that sacrifice is unpleasaunt in thy sight/ whiche is offred in remembraunce
of displeasure or neglygence/ of reconcylyng his brothers good
wyll. Therfore thy sonne gaue vs this in commaundement/ that
we shulde leaue our offring euyn at the auter/ and hye vs a pace
to our brother/ and labour to be in peace with hym/ and than
returne agayne and offre vp our rewarde: Lawe nowe/ we folowe
that thy sonne hath taught vs/ we endeuer to performe that he
hath done/ if thou aknowlege the couenant and bargayne made of
thy sonne/ as we dout nat but thou doest/ graunt vs we beseke
the/ that thyng wherof we had full hope and trust by thy sonne:
Thus he bad vs praye whan he answered nat a fewe tymes/ that
we shulde optayne whatsoeuer we desyred of the in his name. He
made vs bolde to pray to the/ vouchesafe thou by him/ to forgyue
those that call vpon the: We aknowlege our owne imbecilite and
feblenesse/ wherby we well perceyue/ into howe shamfull and
abhomynable offences we were lyke to fall into/ except we were
preserued by thy goodnesse from gretter synnes: and the same
mekenesse thou leftest in vs/ as a remedy against the pride which
we shulde haue ben in ieopardy to haue fallen in dayly: We offende
and fall/ to the entent that euery daye we might glorify thy gentylnesse: Graunt father that we may hertely forgyue our bretherne/
that whan we be in peace and vnite amongest ourselfes/ we may
haue the alway mercyfull vnto vs/ and if in any thyng we offende
the/ amende vs with thy fatherly correction/ so that thou vtterly

forsake vs nat/ nor disinherite vs/ ne cast vs into hell; ones in baptyme thou hast remytted vs all our synnes/ but that was nat inoughe/ for thy tendre loue towarde vs/ but thou hast also shewed a sure and redy remedy/ for the dayly offences of thy children/ for the whiche we thanke thy great gentylnesse/ whiche vouchesauest by thy sonne and the holy gost/ to endewe vs with so great benifytes to the euerlastyng glorie of thy moost holy name. Amen.

The sixte peticion.

Et *ne nos in ducas in tentationem.* O good father in heuen/ albeit there is nothing that we greatly feare/ hauyng the mercy-full vnto vs/ and whyle mutuall loue and charyte eche with other/ maketh vs thy children of more strength agaynst euery yuell assaut/ yet whan we consydre howe weake and fraile the nature of man is/ and howe ignorant also we be/ whome thy goodnesse wyll iudge and thynke worthy the contynuaunce in thy loue/ to the ende of this lyfe/ in whiche as long as we are/ a thousande maner of wayes we be stered to fall and ruyne/ therfore we can nat be vtterly seker and carelesse: all this lyfe is roundeabout be sette with the dyuelles snares/ he neuer cesseth temptynge vs/ whiche was nat afrayde with craftie subtylteis to sette vpon thy sonne Jesus/ We call to mynde how greuously the fende assuated thy seruaunt Job: We remembre howe Saull was fyrst thy electe and chosen seruaunt/ and within awhile after cast out of thy sight: We can nat forget howe Dauyd whom thou calleddest a man euyn after thyne owne appetyte/ was drawen to that great villany of synne/ that he mengled aduoutre with manslaughter: We consydre howe Solomon whom in the begynnyng of his rule/ thou gauest wysedome aboue all men/ was brought to that madnesse and folly/ that he dyde sacrifyce to strange and vtter goddes: We remembre also/ what befell the chefe and heed of thyne apostles/ whiche after that he had so valyantly professed/ that he wolde dye with his mayster/ natwithstandyng thrise forsware his maister. These and suche many other/ whan we consydre/ we can nat but feare and aborre the ieopardy of temptacion: and thy fatherly loue wolde vs alway to be in this feare/ bycause we shulde nat sluggisshely and slouthfully begyn to trust in our owne helpe/ but

defende and arme ourselfe agaynst euery saute of temptacion with
sobre temperaunce/ watche/ and prayer: wherby we shulde neyther prouoke our ennemy/ remembring our owne feblenesse/ nor
be ouerthrone in the storme of temptacion trustyng to thy ayde/
without whiche we are able to do right nought/ thou suffrest among
temptacion to fall/ eyther to proue and make stedfast the suffraunce and pacience of thy children/ as Job and Abraham were
tempted/ or els by suche scourges to correcte and chasten our
offences: but howe often soeuer thou suffrest this /we praye the
thou wylt bring that same temptacion to good and lucky ende/ and
gyue vs strength egall to the mountenaunce and weight of the
yuels that come vpon vs/ it is no lytell ieopardy whansoeuer we
be thretned with losse of our goodes/ with banysshement/ re-
bukes/ imprisonment/ with bandes and bodily turmentyng/ and
horrible and fearfull dethe. But we are in no lesse peryll at all/
whan prosperite to moche laugheth on vs/ than whan we be ouer
moche feared with trouble and aduersyte: They are an innumerable
sorte whiche fall on euery side/ some for feare of punysshment
do sacrifyce to wicked deuyls/ some ouerthrone and astonyed
with yuels and vexacions/ do blaspheme thy most holy name:
and agayne/ some drowned with ouer moche worldely welthe/
sette at nought and dyspice thy gyftes of grace/ and retourne
agayne into their olde and former fylthynesse/ as the sonne that
the scripture speketh of/ whiche after tyme he hadde spent and
reuelled out all his fathers substaunce/ by vnthrifty and vngracious
rule/ was brought, to that misery and wretchednesse/ that he
enuyed the swyne their chaffe. We knowe well good father/ that
our aduersary hath no power ouer vs at all/ but by thy suffraunce:
Wherfore we be content to be put to what soeuer ieopardy it
pleaseth the/ so it wyll lyke thy gentylnesse to measure our en-
nemys assaute and our strength/ for so though we be somtyme in
the fyrst metyng to weake/ yet thy wysedome in the conclusyon
wyll tourne it to our welthe. So thy most dere and honorable son/
was euer wonte to ouercome the deuyll: thus the flesshe: and
thus the worlde: that whan he semed moost to be oppressed/
he than moost specially triumphed/ and he fought for vs/ he
ouercame for vs/ and triumphed for vs: Let vs also ouercome by
his ensample with thy helpe/ and by the holy goost/ procedyng
from bothe foreuer. Amen.

The seuenth peticion.

S *ed libera nos a malo.* O almyghty father/ it hath pleased thy mere and liberall goodnesse/ ones whan we were rydde from synne/ to delyuer vs by thy sonne Jesus Christ/ out of the handes of our moost foule and vnclene father the deuyll/ and to electe and take vs into the honour bothe of thy name and thyne inherytaunce: but yet of this condycion that all the while we lyue here in erthe we shulde be in contynuall batell with our enemy/ whiche leaueth no wayes vnassayed/ wherby he might drawe and plucke vs agayne into his power and authorite/ we quake and trymble in herte/ as often tymes as we remembre howe shamefull a father we had/ whan we were thrall and bonde to synne/ and to howe wretched and vnhappy interitaunce we were apoynted/ and howe currysshe and vngentyll a mayster we serued. And we knowe well inoughe/ his obstinate and frowarde malice and yuell wyll/ whiche alwaye layeth wayte and lyeth redy bent to our distruction/ nat onely with violence and stronge hande/ but also with traynes and subtell wyles/ he neuer slepeth nor resteth/ but alway ronneth vp and downe hyther and thyther lyke a rauenous lyon/ lyeng in wayte/ sckynge and huntyng about/ whom he maye deuoure. Verily father he is farre vnlyke the/ for thou art naturally good and gentyll/ thou caryest home agayne to the flocke/ the wandringe and strayeng shepe: thou curest and makest hole the sicke and scabbe shepe/ and releuest the deed: ye/ and thyne ennemyes also/ and blasphemers of thy holy name thou preuentest with thy loue/ and callest moost graciously to euerlastyng helthe: But he of an vnreasonable and vnsacyable hatered towarde vs/ which neuer dyde hym displeasure/ laboureth and gothe about nothyng elles/ than to bringe with hym as many as he can into distruction: It is a signe and token of an excedynge malyce/ one for nought and without any commodyte of his owne/ to endeuer to distroy hym of whom he was neuer wronged/ but this euyn with his owne hurte/ wayteth those hurt and domage/ whome thou hast taken asyde vnder thy protection: thou madest hym nat suche but he fyll into this great malyce/ after tyme he begon to stande in his owne conceyt/ and refused to be subiet and obedyent to thy maiestie: Wherfore he beyng pricked all with enuy/ by crafty besegyng/ entysed to distruction our firste progenytours/ enuyeng them the ioyes of paradyse/ for as moche as he had de-

priued hymselfe of the gladnesse and myrthe of heuen/ but nowe
he is of farre greater enuy/ bicause thou cariest them out of para-
dyse into heuen: and whereas they were afore apoynted to dethe
and dampnacton/ thou by reason of the faythfull trust whiche they
haue put in thy sonne Jesus/ callest them to euerlastyng blysse:
and also/ that thou tournest his owne malyce into th encrease of
thy glorie and our helthe: Wherfore thoughe nat without a cause/
he is of many to be feared: yet thy goodnesse dothe conforte vs/
whiche is able to do more to our helthe and saluacion/ than all his
malyce to our distruction. We aknowlege our owne imbecilite and
feblenesse/ but yet we feare nat our ennemyes assaute/ whyther
we lyue or dye/ all the whyle we deserue to haue the our protectour
and defender/ We feare no dystruction of that yuell and wicked
deuyll/ all the whyle it is our chaunce to stycke to hym that is
so good. These desyres and petycions of thy chyldren/ O immortall
father/ if they be good and after the forme and order apoynted of
thy sonne Jesus/ than we nothyng mystrust/ but that thou wylte
performe that whiche we desyre of the. Amen.[1]

Thus endeth the exposicion of the Pater noster. Imprinted at
London in Fletestrete/ in the house of Thomas Berthelet nere to
the Cundite/ at the signe of Lucrece.

Cum priuilegio a rege indulto.

---

[1] A modern, but imperfect, transcription of the seventh petition was reprinted by Ernest E. Reynolds in *Margaret Roper. . . .* (London: Burns
& Oates, 1960), pp. 41–43.

Footnotes

ERASMUS OF ROTTERDAM IN PROFILE

1. Peter Gay, *The Enlightenment: An Interpretation* (New York: Alfred A. Knopf, 1967), p. 274.

2. The date of Erasmus's birth has been the subject of considerable debate. For a discussion of the controversy, see Albert Hyma, *The Youth of Erasmus*. Second ed. (New York: Russell & Russell, 1968), p. 51.

3. Johann Huizinga, *Erasmus of Rotterdam* (London: Phaidon Press, Ltd., 1952), p. 5.

4. *Ibid.,* pp. 8–9.

5. For an account of the origins and history of the *Devotio Moderna,* see Albert Hyma, *The Christian Renaissance.* Second ed. (Hamden, Connecticut, 1965).

6. A. Hyma, *The Youth of Erasmus,* pp. 167–204.

7. Preserved Smith, *Erasmus: A Study of His Life, Ideals and Place in History* (New York: Harper & Brothers, 1923), pp. 25–26.

8. Margaret Mann Phillips, *Erasmus and the Northern Renaissance* (London: Hodder & Stoughton Ltd., 1949), p. 6.

9. J. Huizinga, *Erasmus of Rotterdam,* p. 22.

10. Craig R. Thompson, "Erasmus as Internationalist and Cosmopolitan," *Archiv für Reformationsgeschichte,* Vol. 46 (1955), pp. 167–95.

11. M. M. Phillips, *Erasmus and the Northern Renaissance,* pp. 32–33.

12. J. Huizinga, *Erasmus of Rotterdam,* pp. 64–65.

13. M. M. Phillips, *Erasmus and the Northern Renaissance,* pp. 60–61.

14. P. S. Allen, *Opvs Epistolarvm Des. Erasmi Roterodami* (Oxford: Clarendon Press, 1958), Vol. 12.

15. J. Huizinga, *Erasmus of Rotterdam,* p. 67.

16. D. Erasmus, *The Praise of Folly,* ed. by Hoyt H. Hudson (Princeton University Press, 1941), p. 68.

17. *Ibid.,* pp. 76–77.

18. Donald B. King and H. David Rix, eds., *Desiderius Erasmus . . . On Copia of Words and Ideas* (Milwaukee, Wisconsin: Marquette University Press, 1963), p. 2.

19. M. M. Phillips, *Erasmus and the Northern Renaissance,* p. 73.
20. C. R. Thompson, "Erasmus as Internationalist and Cosmopolitan," pp. 176–177.
21. P. Smith, *Erasmus,* p. 341.
22. Roland H. Bainton, *Erasmus of Christendom* (New York: Charles Scribner's Sons, 1969), pp. 236–37. Bainton incorrectly dates Metsys's portrait of Erasmus as 1519.
23. P. Smith, *Erasmus,* pp. 203–208.
24. J. Huizinga, *Erasmus of Rotterdam,* pp. 174–75.
25. P. Smith, *Erasmus,* pp. 417–19.

ERASMUS THE HUMANIST

1. Gerhard Ritter, "Lutheranism, Catholicism and the Humanistic View of Life," *Archiv für Reformationsgeschichte* (44; 1954), 145–59.

2. Lorenzo Valla, *Dialogue on Free Will,* tr. Charles E. Trinkhaus Jr., in *The Renaissance Philosophy of Man,* ed. Ernst Cassirer, Paul Oskar Kristeller, & John Herman Randall Jr. (Chicago: Phoenix Books, 1948), pp. 155–84.

3. A study once done by the present writer found that of the German, Dutch, and Swiss humanists born between 1450 and 1480 only 5 of 24 became Protestants; of those born between 1481 and 1510 84 of 127 became Protestants.

4. *De Libero Arbitrio, Opera Omnia Des Erasmi,* ed. J. Leclercq (10 vols.; Lugduni Batavorum: 1703–1706) [this edition hereafter referred to as LB], vol. IX, 1215–48. Erasmus's sources are discussed in Pierre Mesnard, *De Libre Arbitre* (Paris: Presses Universitaires de France, 1945), and Ernst W. Kohls, "La Position Théologique d'Erasme et la Tradition dans le *De Libero Arbitrio,*" *Colloquim Erasmusnum: Actes du Colloque International réuni à Mons.* (Mons: Centre Universitaire d'Etat, 1968), pp. 69–88.

5. Paul O. Kristeller, "The Humanist Movement," *Renaissance Thought: The Classic, Scholastic and Humanist Strains* (New York: Harper Torchbooks, 1961), pp. 3–24. See also his "Humanism and Scholasticism in the Italian Renaissance," *ibid.,* pp. 92–120, and "Humanist Learning in the Italian Renaissance," *Renaissance Thought II* (New York: Harper Torchbooks, 1965), pp. 1–20.

6. For a summary of the arguments between rhetoric and philosophy see Werner Jaeger, *Paideia: The Ideals of Greek Thought,* vol. III, chapter II, "Socrates the Teacher." For the two sides, Plato's *Gorgias* and Isocrates' *Antidosis* (Loeb Classical Library edition of the Orations of Isocrates, vol. II, esp. pp. 337–39).

7. Aubrey Gwynn, S.J., *Roman Education from Cicero to Quintilian* (Oxford: Clarendon, 1926); Cicero, *De Oratore*, 1.6.

8. *De Oratore*, III.76; *De Inventione*, 1.2 (in a more mature work Cicero credits philosophy rather than rhetoric with this accomplishment—*Tusculanae Disputationes* V.5—but by this time rhetoric and philosophy have been joined together: see note 14).

9. *Tusculanae Disputationes* II.2, IV.3.

10. See note 5, "The Humanist Movement," p. 11.

11. Seneca, *Epistulae Morales*, LXXIII.15–6; Cicero, *Tusculanae*, III.2.

12. Plato, *The Republic*, #439; Cicero, *De Officiis* I. 14 (honor); I.15, 18–19 (gentle virtues).

13. Quintilian, *Institutionis Oratoriae Libri XII*, I.iii.8–14.

14. Jerrold E. Seigel, *Rhetoric and Philosophy in Renaissance Humanism* (Princeton University Press, 1968); Paul Joachimsen, "Loci Communes: Eine Untersuching zur Geistesgeschichte des Humanismus und der Reformation," *Luther Jahrbuch* (VIII; 1926), 27–97.

15. For studies and source works on humanist pedagogy in Italy, see William H. Woodward, *Vittorino da Feltre and other Humanist Educators* (New York: Columbia Teachers College, 1964); Eugenio Garin, *Il Pensiero Pedagogico dello Umanesimo* (Florence: Giustine & Sansoni, 1958); and Sister Maria Walburg Fanning and Sister Anne Stanislaus Sullivan, *Maffei Vegii De Educatione Liberorum Libri VI* (2 vols; Washington: Catholic University Press, 1933–36).

16. *Elegantiarum Linguae Latinae Libri VI, Laurentii Vallae Opera* (Basel: Heinrich Petri, 1540), pp. 4, 80.

17. *Lorenzo Valla's Treatise on the Donation of Constantine*, tr. Christopher B. Coleman (New York: Yale University Press, 1922); Max von Wolff, *Lorenzo Valla, sein Leben und seine Werke* (Leipzig: E. A. Seemann, 1893), pp. 62 ff. (Erasmus followed Valla's argument on the Apostles' Creed: *Apologia Brevis ad . . . Libros Alberti Pii*, LB IX 1170AB); Valla's notes to the New Testament are printed in *Vallae Opera Omnia* (2 vols.; Turin: Bottegha d'Erasmo, 1962), vol. I.

18. Richard McKeon, "Renaissance and Method in Philosophy," *Columbia University Studies in the History of Ideas* (III, 1933).

19. P. S. Allen, *Opus Epistolarum Des. Erasmi Roterodami* (Oxford: Clarendon, 1906–58; 12 vols.), Letters 10–15, vol. I.

20. Letters 22 and 11; "Apologia Erasmi et Cornelii adversus Barbaros," Cornelius Reedijk, *The Poems of D. Erasmus* (Leiden: Brill, 1956), pp. 162 ff. The 1494 version of *Antibarbarorum Liber* is edited by Albert Hyma, *The Youth of Erasmus*. Second ed. (New York: Russell & Russell, 1968).

21. *De Duplici Copia Rerum ac Verborum,* not published until 1512; also *De Ratione Studii,* published in 1511. Both are found in LB I. There were also early versions of *De Conscribendis Epistolis* and *Familiarum Colloquiorum Formulae.*

22. Notably *De Pueris statim ac liberaliter Instituendis,* recently edited by Jean Claude Margolin (Geneva: Droz, 1966).

23. P. N. M. Bot, *Humanisme en Onderwijs in Nederland* (Utrecht: Het Spectrum, 1953), 62–63.

24. *De Pueris . . Instituendis,* LB I, 504E–505A.

25. See P. S. Allen, *The Age of Erasmus* (Oxford: Clarendon, 1914) pp. 36–40 for this sample from John of Garland's *Textus Equivocorum.* Valla's list of bad textbooks (*Elegantiae,* p. 41) is similar to Erasmus's (Letter 26, I, pp. 114–15).

26. Letter 64, 1. 190–93; Letter 23, 1. 81–100; *Conflictus Thaliae ac Barbariei,* LB I 892AF; Letter 56, 1. 17–19.

27. E.g., *Jean Gerson: Ouevres Complètes,* ed. Msgr. Glorieux (Paris: Desclee, 1960), vol. I, 34; Christian Dolfen, *Die Stellung des Erasmus zur Scholastischen Methode* (Osnabrück: Meinders & Elster-mann, 1936), pp. 30 ff., comments on similarities between Erasmus's position and the *theologia practica* of later medieval writers like Gerson. For his expectations of scholastics, see *Antibarbarorum Liber,* ed. Hyma, pp. 258–60; Letter 943, 1. 83–93, III, 543; Letter 1581, 1. 436–53, VI, 98.

28. *De Conscribendis Epistolis* (Basel: John Froben, 1522), pp. 7, 12–13; Letter 447, 1. 87–91, II, 295.

29. *Antibarbarorum Liber,* p. 307: "Est enim huic scriptorum generi moris nichil suum ponere, sed diversorum dicta hinc inde decerpta congere, non mode diversa, sed inter se pugnantia: sat habent coaceruasse, ceterum iudicii onus lectori relinquentes." The speaker does not seem to realize that the opinions gathered for the purpose of stimulating debate are supposed to be contrary. For humanist dialectic, see Walter J. Ong, S. J., *Ramus, Method, and the Decay of Dialogue* (Cambridge: Harvard University Press, 1962).

30. Erasmus does not say that the study of dialectic in itself makes people narrow and argumentative, but cf. the passage from letter 1581 cited above, note 27. On fulminating against married clergy (of whom Erasmus's father was one) see *Antibarbarorum Liber,* p. 276; Letter 858, 1. 417–24, III, 372; Letter 1188, 1. 8–13, IV, 447.

31. *Oratio de Pace,* LB VIII, 547AB.

32. Letters 10–14; *The Republic,* #398–402; Jean Claude Margolin, *Erasme et la Musique* (Paris: Vrin, 1965). The best study of Erasmus's pedagogy is William H. Woodward, *Desiderius Erasmus*

concerning the Nature and Aims of Education (Cambridge University Press, 1904).

33. Letter 56, 1. 24–27, I, 172; *De Ratione Studii, LB* I, 521CD; Quintilian, I.iii.8, II.xiii.1–2; *De Conscribendis Epistolis* (Cambridge: John Siberch, 1521), sig. Civ-Div.

34. Quintilian, X.iii.10–8; Cicero, *De Oratore,* I.33; Pier Paolo Vergerio, in Woodward, *Vittorino da Feltre,* p. 99; *Maffei Vegii De Educatione,* p. 79.

35. Letter 15, 1. 24–46, I, 89.

36 *Antibarbarorum Liber,* pp. 257–60; cf. the letter *De Formando Studio* in *Rodolphi Agricolae Phrisii Lucubrationes Aliquot* (Cologne: Joannes Gymnicus, 1532), sig. Bb⁴–Dd².

37. Allen I, 37, 1. 2–10; Letter 604, III, 16; Letter 2189, VIII, 217.

38. Letter 152, I, 355; Letter 182, p. 406.

39. Bot (see note 23), pp. 77–119; R. R. Bolgar, *The Classical Heritage and its Beneficiaries* (New York: Harper Torchbooks, 1964), pp. 329–68.

40. *De Pueris Instituendis, LB* I, 504CD: but the preference for town schools is at the expense of schools run by the Brethren of the Common Life rather than at the expense of private tutors.

41. Letters 111, 163-65.

42. Letters 179, 180, I, pp. 395–403; *Ad . . Principem Phillipum Panegyricus, LB* IV, 507–50.

43. Letters 181, 205, 207–212; Augustin Renaudet, *Erasme et l'Italie* (Geneva: Droz, 1954).

44. Letters 384, 396. Erasmus's New Testament scholarship is evaluated by A. Bludau, *Die beiden ersten Erasmus-Ausgaben des neuen Testaments und ihre Gegner* (Freiburg: Herder, 1902) and Bo Reicke, "Erasmus und die Neutestamentliche Rextgeschichte," *Theologische Zeitschrift* (1966), 254–65.

45. Allen, I, 229, 373.

46. *Enchiridion Militis Christiani, LB* V, 40CD. On peace: Letter 288, I, pp. 551–54; the Adage "Dulce Bellum Inexpertis," translated in Margaret Mann Phillips, *The Adages of Erasmus* (Cambridge University Press, 1964); *Querela Pacis, LB* IV, 625–42.

47. Opinions falsely claimed as dogmas included: that the sacrament of confession as currently practiced (private, auricular confession) was instituted by Christ or practiced by the Apostles (*Exomologesis, LB* V, 145C—146A); that marriage is not dissoluble (note to 1 Cor. 7 in *Annotationes in N. T.,* 1519 edition, pp. 325–334); and that the pope exercised his authority *de jure divino* (*Ad Blasphemias Stunicae, LB* IX, 370EF; *Ad Censuras Facultatis,* 920BD, 1087CD). Erasmus's position on *consensus Ecclesiae* as the source of authority is

shown by Georg Gebhardt, *Die Stellung des Erasmus von Rotterdam zur Römischen Kirche* (Marburg: R. F. Edel, 1966), pp. 52–58.

48. Free will and predestination: *Supputatio in Errores Beddae,* LB IX, 639A; *Ecclesiastes,* V, 781DE. The Eucharist: Letter 2853, 1. 46–58, X, 283. Arianism: *Responsio ad Notulas Beddaicas,* LB IX, 717DE–718B (defending one of his annotations to Jerome's dialogue *Adversus Luciferianos,* in which he said the Arians were superior to their opponents in learning and eloquence, and that their movement was a schism rather than a heresy); he believed, as he thought the (Semi-) Arians did, that only the Father could in a strict sense be called *principium absolutum* (Ad Notationes Lei, LB IX, 184A–188F, 252E); *homoousion* was a "res indigna" to have caused so much controversy (*ibid.,* 271C–272BC).

49. Note to Matt. 11:30, *Annotationes in N.T.,* 1519, pp. 43–44; *Convivium Religiosum, familiarum Colloquiorum Formulae* (Basel: Froben, March 1523), sig. K5ᵛ–7; *Novum Instrumentum* (1516), note to Luke 22:38, and *Querela Pacis,* Lb IV, 635CD.

50. Augustin Renaudet, *Etudes Erasmiennes* (Paris: E. Droz, 1939); Louis Bouyer, *Autour d'Erasme* (Paris: Cerf, 1955). Views similar to Renaudet's are held by Lamberto Borghi, *Umanesimo e Concezione Religiosa in Erasmo di Rotterdamo* (Florence: G. C. Sansoni, 1935); W. Koehler, "Erasmus als religiöse Persönlichkeit," *Bijdragen voor Vaderlandsche Geschiedenis en Oudheidkunde* (VII–7, 1936), pp. 213–25; Joseph Lortz, "Erasmus—Kirchengeschichtlich," *Aus Theologie und Philosophie: Festschrift für F. Tillmann,* ed. T. Steinbüchel & T. Müncker, (Düsseldorf, 1950), pp. 271–326; and Eugene Rice, "Erasmus and the Religious Tradition, 1495–1499," *Journal of the History of Ideas* (XI, 1950), pp. 387–411.

51. Ernst Wilhelm Kohls, *Die Theologie des Erasmus* (2 vols.; Basel: Friedrich Reinhardt, 1966. Gebhardt (note 47) would agree with Kohls. Similar but more nuanced judgments are found in Johannes Lindeboom, *Erasmus: Onderzoek naar zijn Theologie* (Leiden: A. H. Adrian, 1909); Alfons Auer, *Die Vollkommene Frömmigkeit eines Christen* (Düsseldorf: Patmos, 1954) and Jacques Etienne, *Spiritualisme Erasmien et Théologiens Lovanistes* (Louvain: Publication Universitaires, 1956).

52. The clearest evidence of how strongly Erasmus believed that doctrine could be tested by morals comes in his negative judgment of the Swiss and South German Reformation: Karl Heinz Ölrich, *Der späte Erasmus und die Reformation* (Münster: Aschendorff, 1961).

53. Letter 181, 1. 46–50, I, 405.

54. Letter 296, 1. 72–87. I, 567–68; *Enchiridion,* LB V, 32DE.

55. *Enchiridion,* LB V, 33A–36A.

56. *Enchiridion,* 37A, 31CF; "Miles et Carthusianus," *Familiarum Colloquiorum Formulae* (Basel: Froben, March 1523), pp. 5ᵛ ff.

57. *Enchiridion,* 6F–8D, 31E–32A; Letter 384, 1. 46–49, II, 185; *Paraclesis,* in Hajo & Annemarie Holborn, *Des. Erasmus Ausgewählte Werke* (Munich: C. H. Beck, 1933), p. 146.

58. *Novum Instrumentum* (1516). p. 341 [called 241].

59. *Paraclesis* (note 57), p. 142.

60. See notes 31 and 49.

61. Letter 109, I, 251–52. Later Erasmus acknowledged that Christ had shown anger but regarded this as an imperfection: *Ad Blasphemias Stunicae,* LB IX, 362BF; *Supputatio, ibid.,* 444B. Cf. *Enchiridion,* LB V, 18F.

62. On Christian liberty, see *Enchiridion,* LB V, 35BE; *Enarratio in Psalmum 1. ibid.,* 181CE; *Paraphrasis D. Erasmi in Epistolas Pauli . . . ad Romanos, Cortinithios & Galatas* (Basel: Froben, 1520), pp. 370–71 (to 2 Cor. 3:15). *Paraclesis* (note 57), pp. 143–44.

63. Auer and Etienne, both very able scholars (note 51), believe that the focal point of Erasmus's attack on ceremonies was his neo-Platonist denigration of matter. But in view of the way Erasmus describes the evil effects of ceremonies (note 55) and in view of the nature of the reform proposals he makes (e.g. not that fasting be abolished but that Christians not be bound to fast under pain of sin: *De Esu Carnium,* LB V, 1202A; "Ichthuophagia," *Fam. Colloquiorum Formulae* [Basel: Froben, 1526], pp. 477, 490), a case can be made that he objected more to the binding nature of ceremonies than to their physical character.

64. Letter 541, II, pp. 487–90.

65. *The Praise of Folly,* tr. Hoyt Hopewell Hudson (Princeton University Press, 1944), pp. 22–23, 38–40 (contrast *Enchiridion,* LB V, 39A); Karl Schaetti, *Erasmus von Rotterdam und die Roemische Kurie* (Basel: Helbing & Lichtenhahn: 1954). pp. 18, 26–27.

66. He is particularly outspoken in Letter 858, to Paul Wolz (III, pp. 361–77) and in the notes to the 1519 edition of his New Testament.

67. For a rejection of pious fraud, see *Vita Hieronymi Stridonensis,* in Wallace Ferguson, *Epuscula Erasmi* (The Hague: Nijhoff, 1933): *Ecclesiastes,* LB V, 776E: "Est enim vere, ut ait ille, bellua multorum capitum omnis populus;" 1522 edition of *Ratio Verae Theologiae* in Holborns, *Ausgewählte Werke,* pp. 206–207.

68. Thomas N. Tentler, "Forgiveness and Consolation in the Religious Thought of Erasmus," *Studies in the Renaissance* (12, 1965). p. 133, citing Eva M. Jung in *Journal of the History of Ideas,* 1943.

69. See the Adages "Auris Batava" and "Herculeis Labores" trans-

lated from the 1508 edition in Phillips (note 46), pp. 210–11, 195–204.

70. On Colet's views and Erasmus's reaction, see Reedijk, *The Poems of Erasmus*, pp. 121, 212; Allen, I, 6, 1. 28–32.

71. *Paraclesis, Ausgewählte Werke*, pp. 139–40: "quo simplior, hoc efficacior est oratio."

72. *Ciceronianus*, LB I, 974A–978E (contrast Letter 108, 1. 19–36, I, 246—47); *Ecclesiastes*, LB V, 983AD (this manual on preaching, written over a period of ten years or more and finally published in 1535, contains both hopeful and skeptical passages about the value of rhetoric, some of the latter possibly dating from the period 1506–1509); *Supputatio*, LB IX, 531BC.

73. Letter 694, 1. 45—56, III, 117—18 (Pfefferkorn) Letter 1166, 1.85, IV, 399 (Aleander); Letter 872, 1. 11–21; Letter 948, 1. 27–36; Letter 962, 1. 25–30; Letter 991, 37–47; Letter 1040, 1. 1–9; Letter 1113, 1. 3–4. For Erasmus's conventional anti-Semitism, see Werner Gundersheimer, "Erasmus, Humanism, and the Christian Cabala," *Journal of the Warburg and Courtauld Institutes* (XXVI; 1963), pp. 38–52.

74. Letter 1156, 1. 8–9; Letter 1167, 1. 72–81; Letter 1225, 191–96; Letter 1228, 1. 25; Letter 1259, 1. 6–7; Letter 1342, 1. 704–19.

75. Letter 1218, 1. 1–2; Letter 1168, 1. 12–14; Letter 1199, 1. 6–7; Letter 1522, 1. 47–54; Letter 2136, 26–40.

76. *Ecclesiastes*, LB V, 941BF, 942BC, 955F—956A.

77. Robert Stupperich, *Humanismus und die Wiedervereinigung der Konfessionen*, in *Studien des Vereins für Reformationsgeschichte* (Leipzig: M. Heinsius, 1935).

78. In a disappointing conclusion to his perceptive biography, Johann Huizinga, *Erasmus*, tr. F. Hopman (New York: Harper Torchbooks), p. 189, speaks of the feline softness of Erasmus in contrast to the oaken strength of Luther and the white heat of Loyola.

ERASMUS THE REFORMER

1. *Corpus Reformatorum*, XII, 264–71, cited in Karl Hartfelder, *Philipp Melanchthon als Praeceptor Germaniae* (Berlin, 1889), p. 118.

2. Ironically the biography of the brilliant Dutch cultural historian Johan Huizinga, *Erasmus* (New York, 1924), in the Great Hollanders series, revealed and even exaggerated the psychological complexities of Erasmus's personality.

3. Augustin Renaudet, *Erasme, sa pensée religieuse (1518–1521)* (Paris, 1926); *Etudes Erasmiennes (1521–1529)* (Paris, 1939), emphasized the "modernist side of Erasmian thought. Louis Bouyer,

Autour d'Erasme (Paris, 1955); English trans., *Erasmus and his Times* (Westminster, Md., 1959), argues vigorously against Renaudet's interpretation. The Erasmus to Enlightenment line is argued by H. A. Enno van Gelder, *The Two Reformations in the 16th Century* (The Hague, 1961).

4. The special strength of Roland Bainton's new biography *Erasmus of Christendom* (New York, 1969) is that, despite Erasmus's disclaimer that he did not merit the name theologian, the author takes very seriously the religious and theological dimension of Erasmus's thought.

5. Hanna H. Gray, "Valla's *Encomium of St. Thomas Aquinas* and the Humanist Conception of Christian Antiquity," Heinz Bluhm, ed., *Essays in History and Literature* (Chicago, 1965), 37–51, 41. Charles Stinger is writing his Stanford doctoral dissertation on "Ambrogio Traversari and the Revival of Christian Antiquity."

6. See Robert Peters, "Erasmus and the Fathers," *Church History* XXXVI, no. 3 (September, 1967), 254–61.

7. The two key statements of their positions are Wilhelm Dilthey, "Auffassung und Analyse des Menschen im 15. und 16. Jahrhundert," *Gesammelte Schriften* (Stuttgart, 1940), 1–63; Ernst Troeltsch, "Renaissance und Reformation," *Gesammelte Schriften*, IV (Tübingen, 1925), 261–96.

8. The author is currently preparing such a volume for the Library of Protestant Thought published by Oxford U. Press, to be entitled *Christian Humanism in the Reformation*, with key treatises translated into English for the first time. One of the most intelligent essays to date on the general theme is that of Heinz Liebing, "Die Ausgänge des europäischen Humanismus," *Geist und Geschichte der Reformation. Festgabe Hanns Rückert* (Berlin, 1966), pp. 357–76.

9. See Felix Gilbert, "The Renaissance Interest in History," Charles Singleton, ed., *Art, Science, and History in the Renaissance* (Baltimore, 1967), pp. 373–87.

10. The classic definitions of Paul Oskar Kristeller, Hans Baron, and other established scholars are well known. Attention should be called, however, to the brief but brilliant statement by Hanna Holborn Gray, "Renaissance Humanism: The Pursuit of Eloquence," *Journal of the History of Ideas*, XXIV, No. 4 (October–December, 1963), 497–514.

11. Heinz Liebing, "Perspektivische Verzeichnungen," *Zeitschrift für Kirchengeschichte*, III (1968), 290–92, discusses the way in which Melanchthon transmits the humanist *fable convenue* about the Dark Ages to Protestantism.

12. Melanchthon's purely humanist writings are very extensive and

the literature on his role as a humanist and man of learning is most impressive. Peter Fraenkel and Martin Greschat, *Zwanzig Jahre Melanchthonstudium. Sechs Literaturberichte (1945–1965)* (Geneva, 1967), pp. 72–77, "Humanismus, Philosophie, Wissenschaften"; 150–158, "Melanchthon als Humanist und Mann der Wissenschaft." Of special interest are Adolf Sperl, *Melanchthon zwischen Humanismus und Reformation* (Munich, 1959), and Wilhelm Maurer, *Der junge Melanchthon zwischen Humanismus und Reformation,* I, *Der Humanist,* II, *Der Theologe* (Göttingen, 1969). Heinrich Bornkamm states flatly that Melanchthon came to Wittenberg as an Erasmian, "Melanchthons Menschenbild," Walter Elliger, ed., *Phillipp Melanchthon* (Göttingen, 1961), pp. 76–90, 78.

13. *Oratio de variarvm Lingvarum cognitione paranda Petro Mosellano Protegense Avthore Lipsiae in Magna Ervditorvm Corona pronunciata* (Leipzig; 2nd ed., Basel, 1519).

14. *Oratio de studio bonarum literarum atque artium et linguae graecae ac latinae* (Leipzig, 1542); *Oratio de cultu pietatis ac virtutis studiis bonarum artium* (Leipzig, 1545).

15. G. W. Bromiley, *Zwingli and Bullinger,* **XXIV,** Library of Christian Thought (London, 1953), pp. 102–18.

16. *Oratio Philippi Melanchthonis in laudem novae scholae, habita Noribergae in corona doctissimorum virorum et totius ferme Senatus (1526),* Robert Stupperich, ed., *Melanchthons Werke in Auswahl,* III, *Humanistische Schriften* (Gütersloh, 1961), 64; also in the *Corpus Reformatorum,* XI, 106 ff.

17. One of the most complete statements is the treatise *Nobilitas literata, liber unus* (Strassburg, 1549). Of his educational treatises the *Scholae Lavinganae* (Lavingae, 1565), provides a good statement of his curricular planning.

18. *Grammatica Philippi Melanchthonis Latina* (Leipzig, 1560). Rhetorical theory fused beautifully with the concept of the power of the spoken Word of the gospel (*Verbum evangelii vocale*).

19. *Necessarias esse ad omne studiorum genus artis dicendi, Philippi Melanchthonis declamatio (sive: Encomium eloquentiae),* Robert Stupperich, ed., *Melanchthons Werke in Auswahl,* III, *Humanistische Schriften* (Gütersloh, 1961), 44–62; also in the *Corpus Reformatorum,* XI, 50 ff.

20. Joachimus Camerarius, *In partitiones ciceronianas commentatiunculae* (Strassburg, 1560). Johannes Sturm, *De amissa dicendi ratione libri duo. Eiusdem, De Literarvm Lvdis Recte Aperiendis, Liber vnvs* (Lyons, 1542); *Ionnis Sturmii, De vniversa ratione elocutionis rhetoricae libri quattuor* (n.p., 1576?).

21. Johannes Secundus Everaerts, 1511–1536, was the greatest of

the sixteenth-century Dutch Latin poets, famous for his *Basia, Epigrammata*, and *Odae*. On Calvinist poetry, see the old volume by Prosper Tarbé, *Recueil de poésies Calvinistes* (1550–1566) (Reims, 1866). The place of Marot's poetic version of the Psalter at Geneva should be kept in mind. The literature on poetry is copious, such as Jacobus Micyllus, *De re metrica libri tres* (Frankfort, 1539). Sturm promoted poetry in his school.

22. See Melanchthon's *Oratio de dignitate legum* (*1543*), Robert Stupperich, ed., *Melanchthons Werke in Auswahl, III, Humanistische Schriften* (Gütersloh, 1961), 115–21; also in the *Corpus Reformatorum*, XI, 630 ff. Guido Kisch has written on both Erasmus and Melanchthon and law: *Erasmus und die Jurisprudenz seiner Zeit* (Basel, 1960); "Melanchthon und die Juristen seiner Zeit," *Melanges Philippe Meylan*, II (Lausanne, 1963), 135–50; "Melanchthon und die Rechtswissenschaften," *Festschrift für Hans Liermann* (Erlangen, 1964), pp. 87–95; *Melanchthons Rechts- und Soziallehre* (Berlin, 1967).

23. Georg Major, *Vitae Patrum, in usum ministorum verbi . . . repurgatae. Cum praefatione Martini Lutheri* (Wittenberg, 1544).

24. *Corpus Reformatorum*, XX, 703 ff.

25. See Peter Fraenkel, *Testimonia Patrum. The Function of the Patristic Argument in the Theology of Philipp Melanchthon* (Geneva, 1961). Of interest, although not without obvious bias, is Pontien Polman, *L'Élément Historique dans la Controverse religieuse du XVIe Siècle* (Gembloux, 1932).

26. See the recent study of the Bern Zwingli specialist Gottfried W. Locher, "Zwingli und Erasmus," *450 Jahre Zürcher Reformation* (Zurich, 1969), pp. 37–61, especially pp. 46 ff., "Christianismus Renascens"—Erasmische Elemente in Zwinglis Theologie. Joachim Rogge, *Zwingli und Erasmus; die Friedensgedanken des jungen Zwingli* (Stuttgart, 1962), documents the early Erasmian influence.

27. See, for example, Joachim Camerarius, *Praecepta morum ac vitae, accomodata aetati puerili. . . .* (Leipzig, 1551).

28. Willehad Paul Eckert, *Erasmus von Rotterdam Werk und Wirkung*, I (Cologne, 1967), p. 21, speaks of the hostility of the Lutherans and the reserve of the Catholics toward Erasmus until the Enlightenment showed a new and strengthened interest in him, but this is too simple a view. Eckert's two volumes, however, offer a beautiful collection of source materials on the life and influence of Erasmus.

29. A. W. Pollard and G. R. Redgrave, *A Short-Title Catalogue of Books . . . 1475–1640* (London, 1950), lists an impressive array of editions and translations of Erasmus's works for England alone, pp.

227–29, nos. 10436–10510. A single title of a combination volume will have to suffice by way of illustration, Georg Major, ed., *Rhetorices Philippi Melanchthonis et copiae Erasmi tabulae* (Nuremberg, 1561). Of interest on this point is Andreas Flitner, *Erasmus im Urteil seiner Nachwelt* (Tübingen, 1952), which traces the views of Erasmus down to the eighteenth century.

30. An edition of the Erasmus-Melanchthon correspondence still of value is Emil Walter, ed., "Erasmus und Melanchthon I. Briefwechsel zwischen Erasmus und Melanchthon," *Einladungsschrift des Herzoglichen Karls-Gymnasiums in Bernburg* (Bernburg, 1877), 25 pp.

31. Wallace K. Ferguson, ed., *Opuscula* (Leiden, 1933), p. 136, cited in Myron P. Gilmore, *Humanists and Jurists* (Cambridge, Mass., 1963), p. 107, slightly revised.

ERASMUS AND HIS PLACE IN HISTORY

1. Erasmus, *Christian Humanism and the Reformation: Selected Writings*, ed. John C. Olin (New York, 1965), pp. 29–30.

2. Jean Rouschausse, *Erasmus and Fisher, Their Correspondence, 1511–1524* (Paris, 1968), p. 83. See also Margaret Mann Phillips, "Some Last Words of Erasmus," in *Luther, Erasmus and the Reformation*, eds. John C. Olin, James D. Smart, and Robert E. McNally, S. J. (New York, 1969), pp. 90–91, for further comment on this predicament.

3. This is amply covered in one fashion or another in practically every volume on Erasmus. For a good review of Erasmus's relations with Luther and Lutheranism, see C. R. Thompson's introduction to his edition of Erasmus's *Inquisitio de fide* (New Haven, 1950).

4. Erasmus, *Christian Humanism and the Reformation*, p. 17, fn. 36, and Martin Luther, *The Bondage of the Will*, trans. J. I. Packer and O. R. Johnston (London, 1957), p. 74 *et passim*.

5. Margaret Mann Phillips, *op. cit.*, p. 97.

6. Augustin Renaudet, *Erasme et l'Italie* (Geneva, 1954), p. 150.

7. Marcel Bataillon, *Erasme et l'Espagne* (Paris, 1937), p. 760.

8. Rouschausse, *loc. cit.*

9. Preserved Smith, *Erasmus, a Study of His Life, Ideals and Place in History* (repr. ed. New York, 1962), Preface, pp. 159, 323, 441, *et passim*.

10. *Ibid.*, pp. 324–25.

11. *Ibid.*, p. 439.

12. *Ibid.*, Preface and p. 159.

13. Bruce E. Mansfield, "Erasmus in the Nineteenth Century: The

Liberal Tradition," *Studies in the Renaissance,* XV (1968), 193–219.

14. H. A. Enno Van Gelder, *The Two Reformations in the Sixteenth Century* (The Hague, 1961), pp. 143–44.

15. Johan Huizinga, *Erasmus of Rotterdam,* trans. F. Hopman (New York, 1952), p. 188.

16. I. e. Chaps. XII–XIV.

17. *Ibid.,* pp. 115–16.

18. *Ibid.,* p. 142.

19. *Ibid.,* p. 136.

20. Margaret Mann Phillips, *Erasmus and the Northern Renaissance* (London, 1949), Chap. VI.

21. *Ibid.,* pp. 223–24.

22. Roland H. Bainton, *Erasmus of Christendom* (New York, 1969), pp. 67–68 *et passim.*

23. *Ibid.,* p. vii.

24. *Ibid.,* p. 35.

25. *Ibid.,* p. 193.

26. *Ibid.,* pp. 193–96, for example.

27. Huizinga, *op. cit.,* pp. 102, 136, 168.

28. Joseph Lortz, *How the Reformation Came,* trans. Otto M. Knab (New York, 1964), pp. 80–88.

29. See also Margaret Mann Phillips, "Some Last Words of Erasmus," in *Luther, Erasmus and the Reformation,* for some later comment and analysis of this relationship.

30. Augustin Renaudet, *Etudes érasmiennes* (Paris, 1939), Introduction and Chap. IV.

31. *Ibid.,* pp. xxi–xxii.

32. *Ibid.,* p. 122.

33. Renaudet, *Erasme et l'Italie,* pp. xi, 175, 200 ff.

34. Renaudet, *Etudes érasmiennes,* pp. xxi and 260, and *idem, Erasme et l'Italie,* pp. 9, 175, 200, 247.

35. J.-C. Margolin, *Erasme par lui-même* (Paris, 1965), pp. 69–85.

36. *Ibid.,* pp. 76 and 81.

37. *Ibid.,* pp. 84–85. Henri de Lubac, S. J., *Exégèse médiévale,* Second Part, II (Paris, 1964), 468–70, and Myron P. Gilmore, *Humanists and Jurists* (Cambridge, Mass., 1963), p. 133, share Margolin's view.

38. The section on Erasmus in de Lubac's *Exégèse médiévale,* Second Part, II, is on pp. 427–82. For a further statement by Bouyer see his "Erasmus in Relation to the Medieval Biblical tradition," in *The Cambridge History of the Bible,* II, ed. G. W. H. Lampe (Cambridge, 1969), 492–505.

39. Louis Bouyer, *Erasmus and His Times,* trans. F. X. Murphy (Westminster, Md., 1959), pp. 149–50.

40. De Lubac, *op. cit.,* Second Part, II, 479.

THE PLACE OF ERASMUS TODAY

1. R. P. Blackmur, "A Garment of Praise for the Spirit of Heaviness," in *The Good European* (The Cummington Press, 1947), p. 18.

2. To be published in the *Proceedings of the Royal Society of Canada* (1971).

3. See *Erasmus in English* (Toronto, 1970) for a discussion of these celebrations, conferences, and congresses.

4. These figures are based upon the two bibliographies for which we are indebted to J.-C. Margolin: *Douze Années de Bibliographie Érasmienne (1950–1961)* (Paris: Vrin, 1963), and *Quatorze Années de Bibliographie Érasmienne (1936–1949)* (Paris: Vrin, 1969).

5. Jean Rouschausse, *Erasmus and Fisher, Their Correspondence, 1511—1524* (Paris: Vrin, 1968), p. 83. Cf. Olin, p. 65.

6. Quoted by Margolin, *Erasme par lui-même* Paris: Ecrivains de Toujours, 1965).

7. In the prefatory letter to the 1518 edition of the *Enchiridion:* cf. Olin, *Desiderius Erasmus: Christian Humanism and the Reformation* (New York: Harper Torchbooks, 1965), p. 130.

8. Julien Benda, *La Trahison des Clercs,* trans. R. Aldington (New York: Wm. Morrow, 1928).

9. Cf. M. A. Screech, *Etudes rabelaisiennes. Tome II: L'Evangélisme de Rabelais. Aspects de la satire religieuse au XVIe siècle,* Travaux Humanisme et Renaissance, XXXII (Genève: Droz, 1959).

10. Thomas More, Letter to Martin Dorp, *Selected Letters,* ed. E. F. Rogers (New Haven: Yale U.P., 1961), p. 20.

11. From a letter of Erasmus to John Botzheim (Allen, I, 37): M. M. Phillips, *The "Adages" of Erasmus* (Cambridge: University Press, 1964), p. xv.

12. *Opera Omnia* (Leiden ed.), V, 37.

13. I have discussed this more fully in my paper on "Erasmus and the Renaissance Re-discovery of Tradition."

14. In a paper to appear in 1971 in the *Proceedings of the Congress on Medieval Canon Law* (Strasbourg).

15. *English Literature in the Sixteenth Century excluding Drama,* Oxford History of English Literature, vol. III (Oxford: Clarendon Press, 1954), p. 174.

16. *Responsio ad Lutherum,* The Complete Works of St. Thomas

More, vol. 5, ed. J. M. Headley (New Haven: Yale University Press, 1969), p. 311.

17. Olin, *Christian Humanism,* p. 142.

18. See my "On reading More's *Utopia* as Dialogue," *Moreana,* 22 (May 1969), 19–32.

19. Olin, *op. cit.,* pp. 144, 139.

20. M. P. Gilmore, "Erasmus" in the *New Catholic Encyclopedia.*

21. E. R. Curtius, *European Literature and the Latin Middle Ages* (New York: Pantheon, 1953), p. 393.

22. F. O. Matthiessen, *Responsibilities of the Critic.*

23. V. Ivanov, q. Curtius, *op. cit.,* p. 395.

24. In *Ne bos quidem pereat,* in Phillips, *Adages,* pp. 376–80.

Introduction to the *Precatio Dominica*

1 Desiderius Erasmus, *Precatio Dominica* . . . (Basel: Johann Froben, 1523).

2 Johann Huizinga, *Erasmus of Rotterdam.* Trans. by F. Hopman (London: Phaidon Press, 1952), p. 13; Albert Hyma, *The Youth of Erasmus.* Second ed. (New York: Russell & Russell, 1969), p. 142; and Percy S. Allen, *Erasmus: Lectures and Wayfaring Sketches* (Oxford: Clarendon Press, 1934), pp. 96–97.

3 Hyma, *The Youth of Erasmus,* p. 142.

4 Joseph Ames and William Herbert, *Typographical Antiquities* . . . (London, 1785), Vol. 1, p. 167. The entry reads: "Erasmus's treatise vpon the Pater-noster; tourned into English by a young vertuous and well lerned gentlewoman of nineteen yere of age. 1524." The existence of a 1524 edition is also established by Richard Hyrde in his dedicatory epistle, dated October 1, 1524, in which he refers to "the laboure I haue had with it about the printing."

5 E. J. Devereux, *A Checklist of English Translations of Erasmus to 1700* . . . (Oxford: Oxford Bibliographical Society, 1968), p. 25. Also see Arthur W. Reed, "The Regulation of the Book Trade Before the Proclamation of 1538," *Transactions of the Bibliographical Society,* Vol. 15 (1917–1919), pp. 166–69.

6 The approximate date of 1531 has been assigned to this issue because the woodcut border on the title page of the Rylands copy differs from the 1525 edition and is in the state described by McKerrow and Ferguson in the ca. 1531 issue of Erasmus's *De Immensa Dei Misericordia.* See Ronald B. McKerrow and F. S. Ferguson, *Title-page Borders* . . . (London: The Bibliographical Society, 1932), #16, p. 13.

7 For a discussion of the various editions, see E. J. Devereux, "Some Lost English Translations of Erasmus," *Transactions of the Bibliographical Society,* Fifth Series, Vol. 17 (1962), pp. 255–59.

8 Ames and Herbert, *Typographical Antiquities,* Vol. 1, p. 401.

⁹ Edward Hodnett, *English Woodcuts, 1480–1535.* (London: The Bibliographical Society, 1935) #2012, p. 397.

¹⁰ John Burke, *Encyclopaedia of Heraldry* . . . Third edition (London: Henry G. Bohn, 1844), n.p.

¹¹ Hodnett, *English Woodcuts,* #1258, p. 308.

¹² Foster Watson, *Vives and the Renascence Education of Women* (London: Edward Arnold, 1912), p. 14. Watson reprinted an imperfect transcript of Hyrde's letter on pp. 162 to 173.

¹³ Nicholas Pocock, *Records of the Reformation, The Divorce: 1527–1533* (Oxford: Clarendon Press, 1870), Vol. 1, pp. 88–89: "We suppose ye know him well; his name is Richard Herde. He was wont to resort much to me, Stephyn Gardyner, there, and dwelled with Master Chancellor of Duchie." See also: Thomas Stapleton, *The Life and Illustrious Martyrdom of Sir Thomas More,* trans. by Philip E. Hallett (London: Burns, Oates & Washbourne, Ltd., 1928), p. 99. Stapleton suggests that "Gunnell [i.e. William Gonell] was succeeded by Richard Hirt, who taught the grandchildren after the marriage of More's children."

¹⁴ Nicholas Harpsfield, *The Life and Death of Sr. Thomas Moore,* ed. by Elsie V. Hitchcock and R. W. Chambers (London: Early English Text Society, 1932), p. 307.

¹⁵ Pocock, *Records of the Reformation,* Vol. 1, p. 88. In a letter to Thomas Cardinal Wolsey, dated March 23, 1528, Stephen Gardiner and John Foxe described Hyrde as "singularly well learned in physic, in the Greek and Latin tongues. . . ."

¹⁶ Joseph Foster, *Alumni Oxonienses* . . . (Nendeln/ Liechtenstein: Kraus Reprint Ltd., 1968), p. 719. The entry reads: "Hirde, Richard (Herde or Hyrde): B.A. (sup. 8 July), 1519."

¹⁷ "Gardiner and Foxe to Brian Tuke," in John S. Brewer (ed.), *Letters and papers* . . . *Henry VIII* (London: Longmans & Co., 1872), Vol. 4 (Part 2), p. 1812.

¹⁸ Gardiner left posterity a record of Hyrde's misfortune in a letter to Cardinal Wolsey. See Pocock, *Records of the Reformation,* Vol. 1, p. 88.

¹⁹ For a fuller account of Margaret's life, see Ernest E. Reynolds, *Margaret Roper, Eldest Daughter of St. Thomas More* (London: Burns & Oates, 1960).

²⁰ Although it is true that Lady Margaret Beaufort, the mother of Henry VII, had earlier translated both the fourth book of the *Imitatio Christi* in 1504 and Denis de Leeuwis, *Speculum Aureum Animae Peccatricis* into English, she worked from French, rather than Latin, editions of these works. See John K. Ingram (ed.), *The Earliest English Translation of* . . . *De Imitatione Christi* . . . (Early English Text Society), Vol 63 (1908), pp. 259–83. Also see E. A. Axon, "The Lady Margaret As a Lover of Literature" in the *Library,* Second Series, Vol. 8 (1907), pp. 34–41.

²¹ For a discussion of this translation's literary merits, see John A. Gee, "Margaret Roper's English Version of Erasmus' *Precatio Dominica* and the Apprenticeship behind Early Tudor Translation," in *The Review of English Studies,* Vol. 13 (1937), pp. 257–71.

Selected Bibliography

I. Collected Latin Works of Erasmus:
   Omnia Opera Desiderii Erasmi ..., ed. by Beatus Rhenanus.
   Basel: Jerome Froben, 1540–1541. 9 vols. in 6.
   Desiderii Erasmi Roterodami Opera Omnia ..., ed. by Jean
   LeClerc. Leiden: Peter van der Aa, 1703–1706. 10 vols. in 11;
   reissued by Hildesheim: George Olms, 1961 and by London:
   Gregg Press, 1962.
   Omnia Opera Desiderii Erasmi ..., ed. by Cornelis Reedijk *et al.*
   Amsterdam: Koninklijke Nederlandsche Akademie van Weten-
   schappen, 1969. 20 projected vols.
   Erasmi Opuscula ..., ed by Wallace K. Ferguson. The Hague:
   Martinus Nijhoff, 1933.
   Desiderius Erasmus Roterodamus. Ausgewählte Werke ..., ed.
   by Hajo and Annamarie Holborn. Munich: C. H. Beck, 1933.
   Erasmus von Rotterdam, Ausgewählte Schriften, ed. by Werner
   Welzig. Darmstadt: Wissenschaftliche Buchgesellschaft, 1968—.
   8 projected vols.
   Opus Epistolarum Desiderius Erasmi Roterodami, ed. by Percy
   S. Allen, H. M. Allen, H. W. Garrod *et al.* Oxford University
   Press, 1906–1958. 12 vols.
   Erasmi Roterodami Silva Carminum ..., ed. by Charles Ruelens.
   Brussels: T-J. I. Arnold, 1864.
   The Poems of Desiderius Erasmus, ed. by Cornelis Reedijk.
   Leiden: E. J. Brill, 1956.

II. Erasmus in the Vernacular
   A. Ten Major Works in English Translation:
      1. *Adagiorum Collectanea* or *Adages* (1500; revised and en-
         larged from 1508–1536).
         The *Adages* is a collection of classical proverbs with
         explanatory notes. Its purpose was to help those who
         wished to write elegant Latin by providing them with a
         guide to the subject matter of classical literature, arranged
         under appropriate headings.
         a. *The "Adages" of Erasmus,* trans. by Margaret M.
         Phillips. Cambridge: University Press, 1964.

141

    b. *Proverbes or Adages* ..., trans. by Richard Taverner (1569). A facsimile reproduction with an Introduction by De Witt T. Starnes. Gainesville, Florida: Scholars' Facsimiles & Reprints, 1956.

2. *Enchiridion Militis Christiani* or *The Handbook of the Christian Soldier* (1503 and 1518).

    Addressed to the laymen, this handbook sketches Erasmus's concept of the philosophy of Christ. The Christian soldier is encouraged to cultivate those virtues which are in keeping with the spirit of the gospel.

    a. *Handbook of the Militant Christian,* trans. by John P. Dolan. Notre Dame, Indiana: Fides Publishers, 1962.

    b. *The Enchiridion* ..., trans by Raymond Himelick. Bloomington: Indiana University Press, 1963.

    c. *The Enchiridion,* trans by Matthew Spinka in *Advocates of Reform* . . . Philadelphia: Westminster Press, 1953, pp. 295–379.

3. *Moriae Encomium* or *In Praise of Folly* (1511).

    Written in the form of an oration, this biting satire severely criticizes academicians, theologians, scientists, and monks. By so doing, Erasmus contributed mightily to the battle against dogmatism and superstition.

    a. *The Praise of Folly,* trans. by Hoyt H. Hudson. Princeton University Press, 1941.

    b. *Moriae Encomium* ..., trans by John Wilson (London: W. Leak, 1668; ed. by Helen M. Allen (Mrs. P. S.). Oxford: Clarendon Press, 1925; reprinted by Ann Arbor: University of Michigan Press, 1958).

    c. *The Praise of Folie,* trans. by Thomas Chaloner. London: Early English Text Society, 1965.

4. *De Duplici Copia Verborum ac Rerum* or *On Copia of Words and Ideas* (1512).

    Conceived as a thesaurus, this collection of Latin phrases and idioms, culled from the classics, offered the Renaissance learner an opportunity to enrich and enlarge his vocabulary.

    On copia of Words and Ideas ..., trans by Donald B. King and H. David Rix. Milwaukee: Marquette University Press, 1963.

5. *Paraphraseon* . . . *in Novum Testamentum* or *Paraphrases on the New Testament* (1517–1524).

    Erasmus directed these scriptural commentaries to a

Europe at war in an effort to plead for peace. His well intentioned plan, however, met with failure.

The First Tome or *Volume of the Paraphrases of Erasmus Upon the Newe Testamente,* trans. by Nicholas Udall *et al.* London: Edward Whitchurch, 1548 (i.e. 1549) . . . 2 vols.

6. *Institutio Principis Christiani* or *The Education of a Christian Prince* (1516).

   This treatise on government sets forth Erasmus's belief in the educability of man and his preference for an elective monarchy.

   The Education of a Christian Prince, trans. by Lester K. Born. New York: Columbia University Press, 1936.

7. *Querimonia Pacis* or *The Complaint of Peace* (1517).

   An avowed promoter of peace, Erasmus condemned warfare and suggested some practical ways of how to avoid future wars.

   a. *Erasmus and Our Struggle for Peace* . . . , trans. by José Chapiro, Boston: The Beacon Press, 1950, pp. 131–84.

   b. *The Complaint of Peace* . . . , trans. by Thomas Paynell. A facsimile reproduction of the Berthelet edition of 1533 with a modernized version of Paynell's translation, ed. with an Introduction by William J. Hirten. New York: Scholars' Facsimiles & Reprints, 1946 and 1967.

8. *Familiorum Colloquiorum Formulae* or *The Familiar Colloquies* (1518; revised and enlarged between 1519–1533).

   Written in the form of dialogues, the *Colloquies* was originally intended as a handbook to learning Latin, but its effect was considerably greater. This delightfully witty collection of conversations offered the student a running commentary on contemporary events.

   a. *The Colloquies of Erasmus,* trans. by Craig R. Thompson. University of Chicago Press, 1965.

   b. *The Colloquies* . . . , trans. by N. Bailey and ed. by E. Johnson. London: Gibbings & Co., 1900. 3 vols.

9. *De Libero Arbitrio* or *Discourse on Free Will* (1524).

   Erasmus, taking exception to Luther's position, sets forth with calm eloquence a belief in man's free will. He based his defense wholly on scripture and reason.

   Discourse on Free Will. Trans. by Ernst F. Winter. New York: Ungar, 1961.

10. *Opus Epistolarum* or *The Collected Letters of Erasmus* (1484 to 1536).

A prolific writer, Erasmus addressed some two thousand Latin letters to friends and eminent contemporaries. Many of the most important of these letters are to be found in the following collections.

a. *The Epistles of Erasmus [to* 1519] . . . , trans. by Francis M. Nichols. London: Longmans, Green and Co., 1901–1918. 3 vols.; reprinted by New York: Russell & Russell in 1962.

b. *Erasmus and Cambridge: The Cambridge Letters of Erasmus.* ed. by Harry C. Porter and trans. by D. S. F. Thomson, University of Toronto Press, 1963.

B. Principal Biographies and Monographs:

ADAMS, ROBERT P. *The Better Part of Valor; More, Erasmus, Colet, and Vives, on humanism, war, and peace, 1496–1535.* Seattle: University of Washington Press, 1962.

ALDRIDGE, JOHN W. *The Hermeneutic of Erasmus.* Richmond, Virginia: John Knox Press, 1966.

ALLEN, PERCY S. *Erasmus: Lectures and Wayfaring Sketches.* ed. by Helen M. Allen. Oxford: Clarendon Press, 1934.

ALLEN, PERCY S. *The Age of Erasmus; lectures delivered in the universities of Oxford and London.* Oxford: Clarendon Press, 1915; reprinted by New York: Russell & Russell, 1963.

AUER, ALFONS. *Die Vollkommene Frömmigkeit des Christen* . . . Düsseldorf: Patmos, 1954.

AUGUSTIJN, CORNELIUS. *Erasmus en de Reformatie.* . . . Amsterdam: H. J. Paris, 1962.

BAINTON, ROLAND H. *Erasmus of Christendom.* New York: Charles Scribner's Sons, 1969.

BATAILLON, MARCEL. *Érasme et l'Espagne: Recherches sur l'histoire spirituelle du xvie siècle.* Paris: Librairie E. Droz, 1937; 2nd ed.: *Erasmo y España.* Buenos Aires, 1950. 2 vols.

BIETENHOLZ, PETER G. *History and Biography in the Work of Erasmus of Rotterdam.* Geneva: Librairie E. Droz, 1966.

BOISSET, JEAN. *Erasme et Luther: Libre ou serf-arbitre?* Paris: Presses Universitaires de France, 1962.

BOUYER, LOUIS. *Erasmus and the Humanist Experiment.* Trans. by Francis X. Murphy. London: Geoffrey Chapman, 1959.

CAMPBELL, WILLIAM E. *Erasmus, Tyndale, and More.* London: Eyre and Spottiswoode, 1949.

DRUMMOND, ROBERT B. *Erasmus: His Life and Character.* London: Smith, Elder and Co., 1873. 2 vols.

EMERTON, EPHRAIM. *Desiderius Erasmus of Rotterdam.* New York: G. P. Putnam's Sons, 1899.

ÉTIENNE, JACQUES, *Spiritualisme érasmien et théologiens louvanistes. . . .* Louvain: Publications Universitaires de Louvain, 1956.

FLITNER, ANDREAS, *Erasmus im Urteil Seiner Nachwelt . . .* Tübingen: M. Niemeyer, 1952.

FROUDE, JAMES A. *Life and Letters of Erasmus.* London: Longmans & Co., and New York: Charles Scribner's Sons, 1894, 1916, and 1925.

GAUTIER-VIGNAL, LOUIS. *Érasme: 1466–1536. . . .* Paris: Payot, 1936.

HARBISON, E. HARRIS. *The Christian Scholar in the Age of the Reformation.* New York: Charles Scribner's Sons, 1956.

HUIZINGA, JOHANN. *Erasmus of Rotterdam; with a selection from the letters of Erasmus.* Trans. by F. Hopman. New York: Charles Scribner's Sons, 1924; new eds.: London: Phaidon Press, 1952, and New York: Harper, 1957.

HYMA, ALBERT. *The Christian Renaissance; a History of the "Devotio Moderna."* Grand Rapids, Michigan: The Reformed Press, 1924, and New York: Century, 1925; 2nd ed., Hamden, Connecticut: Archon Books, 1965.

HYMA, ALBERT. *The Youth of Erasmus.* Ann Arbor: University of Michigan Press, 1930; 2nd ed.: New York: Russell & Russell, 1968.

JORTIN, JOHN. *The Life of Erasmus. . . .* London: J. Whiston and B. White, 1758–60. 2 vols. Reprinted in 1805, 1808, and 1809.

KAISER, WALTER J. *Praisers of Folly: Erasmus, Rabelais, Shakespeare.* Cambridge: Harvard University Press, 1963, and London: Victor Gollancz, 1964.

KISCH, GUIDO. *Erasmus und die Jurisprudenz seiner Zeit . . .* Basel: Helbing & Lichtenhahn, 1960.

KNIGHT, SAMUEL. *The Life of Erasmus. . . .* Cambridge: Cornelius Crownfield, 1726.

KOHLS, ERNEST W. *Die Theologie des Erasmus.* Basel: Friedrich Reinhardt, 1966. 2 vols.

LINDEBOOM, JOHANNES. *Erasmus; Onderzoek naar zijne the-*

ologie en zijn godsdienstig gemoedsbestaan. Leiden: A. H. Adriani, 1909.

MAJOR, EMIL. *Erasmus von Rotterdam.* Basel: Frobenius. 1930.

MANGAN, JOHN J. *Life, Character, & Influence of Desiderius Erasmus of Rotterdam.* New York: The Macmillan Co., and London: Burns, Oates & Co., 1927. 2 vols.

MARGOLIN, JEAN CLAUDE. *Érasme par lui-même.* Paris: Éditions du Seuil, 1965.

McCONICA, JAMES K. *English Humanists and Reformation Politics under Henry VIII and Edward VI.* Oxford: Clarendon Press, 1965; reprinted with corrections in 1968.

MEISSINGER, KARL A. *Erasmus von Rotterdam.* Wien: Gallus, 1942; 2nd ed.: Berlin: Albert Nauck & Co., 1948.

MESTWERDT, PAUL. *Die Anfänge des Erasmus.* . . . Leipzig: Rudolf Haupt, 1917.

MURRAY, ROBERT H. *Erasmus & Luther: Their Attitude To Toleration.* London: Society for Promoting Christian Knowledge, 1920.

NEWALD, RICHARD. *Erasmus Roterodamus.* Freiburg im Breisgau: Erwin Burda, 1947.

NOLHAC, PIERRE DE. *Érasme en Italie.* . . . Paris: Reenes and C. Klincksieck, 1888 and 1898.

NULLI, SIRO A. *Erasmo e il Rinascimento.* Torino: Guilio Einaudi, 1955.

OELRICH, KARL H. *Der späte Erasmus und die Reformation.* . . . Munster im Westfalen: Aschendorffsche Verlagsbuchhandlung, 1961.

PAYNE, JOHN B. *Erasmus: His Theology of the Sacraments.* Richmond, Virginia: John Knox Press, 1969.

PFEIFFER, RUDOLF. *Humanitas Erasmiana.* Leipzig and Berlin: B. G. Teubner, 1931.

[PHILLIPS], MARGARET MANN. *Érasme et Les Débuts de la Réforme Française* (1517–1536). Paris: Librairie Ancienne Honoré Champion, 1934.

PHILLIPS, MARGARET M. *Erasmus and the Northern Renaissance.* London: Hodder and Stoughton, 1949, and New York: Macmillan, 1950 and 1965.

PINEAU, J.-B. *Érasme: Sa Pensée Religieuse.* Paris: Les Presses Universitaries de France, 1923 and 1924.

POST, REGNERUS R. *The Modern Devotion: Confrontation with Reformation and Humanism.* Leiden: E. J. Brill, 1968.

RENAUDET, AUGUSTIN. *Érasme et L'Italie.* . . . Genève: Librairie E. Droz, 1954.

RENAUDET, AUGUSTIN. *Études Érasmiennes* (1512–1529). Paris: Librairie E. Droz, 1939.

REYNOLDS, ERNEST E. *Thomas More and Erasmus.* London: Burns & Oates, and New York: Fordham University Press, 1965.

RITTER, GERHARD. *Erasmus und der deutsche Humanistenkreis am Oberrhein.* . . . Freiburg im Breisgau: F. Wagner, 1937.

SCHÄTTI, KARL. *Erasmus von Rotterdam und die Römische Kurie.* Basel and Stuttgart: Helbing & Lichtenhahn, 1954.

SCHOTTENLOHER, OTTO. *Erasmus im Ringen um die humanistische Bildungsform.* . . . Munster im Westfalen: Aschendorff, 1933.

SEEBOHM, FREDERIC. *The Oxford Reformers of 1498: being a history of the fellow-work of John Colet, Erasmus and Thomas More.* London: Longmans, Green and Co., 1867; 2nd ed., 1869; 3rd ed., 1887, 1896, 1911; also published by London: J. M. Dent and Sons, 1914 and 1929.

SMITH, PRESERVED. *Erasmus: A Study of His Life, Ideals, and Place in History.* New York: Harper & Brothers, 1923; new ed., New York: Ungar, 1962.

SPITZ, LEWIS W. *The Religious Renaissance of the German Humanists.* Cambridge: Harvard University Press, 1963.

STANGE, CARL. *Erasmus und Julius II.* Eine Legende. Berlin: A. Töpelmann, 1937.

TELLE, ÉMILE V. *Érasme de Rotterdam et Le Septième Sacrement.* . . . Genève: Librairie E. Droz, 1954.

TREINEN, HANS. *Studien zur Idee der Gemeinschaft bei Erasmus von Rotterdam.* Druck: Saarzeitung Saarlouis, 1955.

WACHTERS, HERMAN J. J. *Erasmus van Rotterdam, zijn leven en zijn werken.* Amsterdam: C. L. Langenhuysen, 1936.

WOODWARD, WILLIAM H. *Desiderius Erasmus Concerning the Aim and Method of Education.* Cambridge: University Press, 1904; reprinted by New York: Teachers College Press, Columbia University, 1964.

ZWEIG, STEFAN. *Erasmus of Rotterdam.* Trans. by Eden and Cedar Paul. London: Cassell and Co., and New York: Viking Press, 1934 and 1956; also published by New York: Garden City Publishing Co., 1937.

Index

(The works of Erasmus are listed under his name)

DATE DUE			
NOV 16 1982			
NOV 1 0 1992			
FEB 2 2 1992			
MAY 1 1 1992			
JUN 1992			
GAYLORD			PRINTED IN U.S.A.